BEING PETER

PERMISSION TO LIVE AND LEAD...LOUD AND LARGE

LEE COATE

First paperback edition May 2024

Book cover & design: Dominique Donesing
Website design: Jeremy Bosma
Social Media: Joseph Valenzuela
Editing: Torrie Sorge
Key Takeaways: Lucas DiMarzio

ISBN: 9798324915544

Unless otherwise noted, Scripture quotations are taken
from the Holy Bible, New International Version®, NIV®.
Copyright © 1973, 1978, 1984, 2011

Published by Growmentum Press
http://www.leecoate.com

. . . .

"Lee's *Being Peter* is a game-changer for anyone who has ever felt their intensity was a barrier in their faith journey. Lee masterfully combines profound insights with actionable next steps, making this book a vital resource for leaders! This book is a must-read for anyone looking to understand and support the *Type I* people in their lives, providing both comprehension perspective and the tools needed to thrive in their unique wiring. *Being Peter* is not just another book on leadership; it's a blueprint for embracing who you are and where God has strategically placed you."

RICH BIRCH | *Founder, unSeminary*

. . . .

"Over the past 15+ years, I've had a front-row seat of watching Lee embrace his unique giftedness and personality for leadership. His creativity, communication, and leadership skills channeled through his God-given wiring have not only been a driving force at The Crossing but to hundreds of churches around the country. *Being Peter* is born out of his own learnings and is a must-read for any leader who is ready to lead at the next level."

SHANE PHILIP | *Sr. Pastor, The Crossing, Las Vegas*

. . . .

"If you're navigating how to make sense of your ambition and drive as a follower of Jesus, then *Being Peter* can help! Through compelling storytelling and practical wisdom, Lee illustrates how embracing one's innate qualities can lead to impactful leadership."

BRAD LOMENICK | *Author, H3 Leadership and The Catalyst Leader*

. . . .

The Apostle Peter was known for always putting his foot in his mouth, having a READY, FIRE, AIM approach to life, and having to be rebuked by Jesus. But in Lee's new book, we not only learn the value of this style of living but how to embrace those who live like this... even if it's us!"

RUSTY GEORGE | *Pastor and Author of Friend of God and After Amen*

"As a *Type I* leader, I've always thought that I needed to conform more to the rest of society. Reading *Being Peter* has taught me that I should embrace these qualities because they have allowed me to build a successful business. I'm grateful that Lee has written this to help those leaders who feel misunderstood!"

RYAN PINEDA | *CEO of Pineda Co*

• • • • • • • • • • •

"This book, written by Executive Pastor and President of Growmemtum, Lee Coate, encourages organizations to embrace their "Peter" people. So many organizations attempt to throttle back these types of direct people so they do not run away with the show. This book will encourage organizations, leaders, and individual contributors to embrace their strengths and soar by fully utilizing their spiritual gifts."

TRICIA JUSTICE | *Vice President, Human Resources, BrightView*

• • • • • • • • • • •

"*Being Peter* is unfortunately not good. No, instead it's absolutely fantastic! As someone who has been told to "quiet down" and "chill out" my entire life, Lee's book resonates. If you've been told similar things, you'll find the words in *Being Peter* refreshing and affirming. And the aspects of identity and obedience that form the foundation of this work are crucial. If you are a visionary, a natural leader, or someone with passion, read this book now. And if you know someone like that, read this book to understand them better. You won't be disappointed."

JONATHON M. SEIDL | *Bestselling author of "Finding Rest: A Survivor's Guide to Navigating the Valleys of Anxiety, Faith, and Life"*

• • • • • • • • • • •

"Lee Coate's *Being Peter* is a powerful exploration of embracing our unique qualities rather than conforming to societal norms. Through the lens of Peter's life, Lee delves into the transformative potential of *Type I* nature, urging us to celebrate authenticity and boldness in leadership. This book is a must-read for anyone seeking to unlock their full potential and foster a healthier, more vibrant team culture. Lee's wisdom and insights are sure to spark meaningful conversations and inspire positive change."

ROB HALL | *Founder and Lead Pastor, New North Church*

• • • • • • • • • • •

"Lee's book shares helpful insights about you or someone close to you who's often perceived as too much. Lee's perspective will help you navigate those around you. *Being Peter* invites you not to be afraid of the person you were created to be. Instead of hiding and turning the volume down on you, Lee encourages you to be the best version of yourself. Best part? Even if you don't see yourself in this book, Lee provides beneficial wisdom for seeing, serving, and supporting those in your world who would be described as *Type I*. If you're interested in being a great self-leader and leader of others, this is the book for you."

MIKE FRISCH | *Lead Pastor, Active Church*

• • • • • • • • • •

"Intense. Highly motivated. Turbo-charged. If that describes you, somebody you work with or live with then this book is a must-read. *Being Peter* is a great case study about someone who lived loudly and led boldly. Through his engaging, practical, and insightful style of writing, Lee gives permission for the *Type I's* to embrace, without apology, their God-given wiring. If there was ever a time that we desperately needed courageous and godly *Type I's*... IT IS NOW!"

LANCE WITT | *Founder, Replenish Ministries*

• • • • • • • • • •

"If you've always felt a little different than everyone else and it's made you wonder if God has a place and purpose for you, this is the book for you. In *Being Peter*, Lee has written an actionable, unique, compelling book. He will give you permission to be who God made you to be and do what He made you to do."

VINCE ANTONUCCI | *Author, I Became a Christian and All I Got Was This Lousy T-Shirt, God For The Rest Of Us*

• • • • • • • • • •

"I had the unique privilege of previewing *Being Peter* early on, and can confidently say Lee's wisdom, experience and writing style combine for an impactful read. As someone in an occupation that requires continuous development of my confidence as a leader, this book is exactly the material I seek. Lee is knowledgeable, disarming and encouraging as a writer and I know this book will be instrumental for leaders in all industries."

MOLLY MCMANIMIE | *Agent & Director of Football, Wasserman Media Group*

• • • • • • • • • •

"*Being Peter* masterfully explores the essence of leadership through the lens of *Type I* individuals. The engaging style and deep understanding of leadership dynamics make this a compelling read for current and aspiring leaders alike. I can't wait to take my church staff through it!"

ADAM HENDERSON | *Lead Pastor, Radiant Church VZ*

• • • • • • • • • •

"*Being Peter* gave me the permission I needed to continue to lead the way in which God has designed me to lead. Lee has created a roadmap for leaders who lead with just an extra bit of salt and pepper. I wholeheartedly endorse this book and think it could change the way you lead."

CARLOS WHITTAKER | *Author, How to Human*

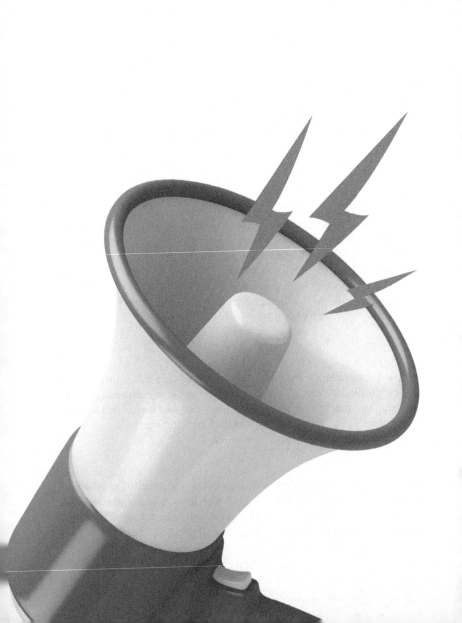

TABLE OF CONTENTS

ACKNOWLEDGMENTS

Embarking on the journey of writing a book is the same as setting out on an adventure into uncharted territories. Crafting a "first" book magnifies this adventure, often resembling an uphill trek filled with challenges. Throughout this endeavor, I found myself ensnared in the fog of stubbornness and procrastination, yet it was the unwavering patience and persistence of those around me that pierced through this haze.

Their relentless encouragement and unwavering affirmation proved indispensable in getting this project across the finish line. It's truly inspiring when individuals invest deeply in something that offers them no immediate reward. Their caring left me deeply inspired... and motivated. For that I am forever grateful.

A heartfelt shout out to Vince Antonucci who was instrumental in the initial shaping of random ideas and primed the pump to start the flow of words. Torrie Sorge's unwavering insistence on completion, coupled with her exceptional editing skills, was instrumental in bringing this project to fruition.

To Shane, Scott, and Kye, my daily collaborators and confidants, who not only endured but embraced my Type I tendencies, providing constant encouragement. My deepest thanks extends to my team at The Crossing Church, who graciously lent their ears to early drafts and bravely served as guinea pigs for my ever evolving ideas.

To my family... the true gold of any life well lived. Ashlee, Austin and my favorite (and only son in law) Mark provide the love, balance and grounding that I desperately need.

Finally, my wife Tanya. You are my person...full of adventure, encouragement and undying support. Building a life with you and in small ways impacting the world God has placed us in fills each day with exhilaration. Thank you for the encouragement and persevering through countless sunrise coffees with my frantic typing providing the background tapping sounds to our otherwise quiet mornings.

And to the *Type I's* that are a part of a deeper circle of friends. Please know that wrestling alongside you with our shared temperaments paralleling our deep faith has been the inspiration for the words that follow.

INTRODUCTION

· · · · · · · · · · ·

I'm a fanboy.

Let's just get that out of the way right up top.

But it's not Taylor Swift, Beyonce, Shohei or Tom Cruise that fires me up. I am a fanboy of someone you might not expect … Simon Sinek.

Who? He is a leadership expert, bestselling author, and TED Talk speaker.

And, I love him. I know. Love is a strong word. I get it. But my confession is vital to us starting on the right foot.

I was attending a conference a few years ago when a friend who helped coordinate the conference sent me a text, "How would you like five minutes with Simon Sinek?" Simon had just finished speaking at one of the main sessions. My response? "When and where? I'll be there."

Simon and I spent five minutes together. Five glorious minutes. He was engaging, asked a lot of questions, and even signed a book for me.

But that's not why I love Simon. Well, it may be part of it.

I love Simon because of the simple yet unparalleled question he asked in his widely viewed TED Talk and bestselling book, *Find Your Why*. Simon says, *"Our WHY is our purpose, cause, or belief—the driving force behind everything we do."*

Our clear *WHY* behind everything in life is extremely important. Therefore it is imperative that every initiative, every argument, and every action in our lives should start with what Harvard professor Hermon Leonard calls "question zero" …WHY?

So, because of my love for Simon and mostly because of how freaking important it is for where we're going in the following pages, we should begin there as well.

Let's go ahead and ask it…question zero.

"Why?"

As someone who's spent decades working in churches and the nonprofit sector, I've had the opportunity to interact with all types of people. I've become especially enamored with high-intensity leaders.

Call them Type A, High-D, Enneagram 8 (and probably some 3), Dominant Red, Finders, or Conceivers on the Thinking Wavelength. It doesn't matter what you call them. You either know one of these intense people or you are one yourself.

I've watched these driven, high-capacity individuals struggle to reconcile how they live out their faith with how they're wired. They are leading and changing the world every day, yet they often struggle to reconcile that drive and intensity with their faith.

I should know. I'm one of them.

I wake up every day and the status quo is my enemy. I strive to create change if change isn't happening or isn't happening fast enough for my taste. I constantly evaluate, motivate, and also irritate those living and working alongside me.

My intensity can be exhausting. But it also serves as the fuel that drives everything forward. I am overly motivated, often too loud, constantly moving, full of crazy (and great) ideas, occasionally obnoxious, and always ambitious. I am frustrating to live with and difficult to live without. I *am* the *why*… and perhaps you are too.

I've found it helpful to name it, to name us.

I call us - *Type I.*

Type I is a ready-to-go, ready-to-risk, and ready-to-conquer alternative that encompasses and bleeds into all the various personality types floating around. *Type I* is largely how a particular personality manifests itself in daily life and in leadership.

You may already be familiar with this reality because a *Type I* is staring back at you every morning when you look in the mirror. You see it. I know I do. It's you.

Now I realize you may be thinking the last thing we need is another "type." I get it. But my goal is not to just dissect another personality type, but rather to give you permission. Permission to live fully in the skin of who you were fearfully and wonderfully made to be.

> MY GOAL IS NOT TO JUST DISSECT ANOTHER PERSONALITY TYPE, BUT RATHER TO GIVE YOU PERMISSION.

Now before you say, "But I'm not a *Type I*," and close this book, I ask you to consider that while you may not be a *Type I*, you know one, actually you probably know quite a few. It's your non-stop spouse, your extra-fiery co-worker, or your aggressive boss. They are constantly moving and shaking up the rooms they walk into, the teams they lead, and frankly, every space where they are given access. Maybe you're leading one on your team. Or perhaps you're being led by one. Maybe you are just working alongside them. You might even be married to one. While it's hard for you to relate to a *Type I* approach to life, it's easy to think of someone you interact with regularly. Frankly, it's easy to think of them because they generally make an imprint, both good and bad.

THE WHY OF TYPE I'S

You might be wondering "Why have another type?" It's true *Type I's* have a lot of similarities with Type A personalities. Let's call them close cousins. But I think there are some unique characteristics that are specifically reflected in a *Type I's*.

"I" CENTRIC

When I say "I," I mean me, myself, and... well, you get the idea. I'm not implying that you're narcissistic, but if you're a *Type I*, you possess a deep sense of self-confidence rooted in your natural aptitude for leadership. This self-assurance can sometimes come across as self-centeredness if you're not self-aware. However, as a *Type I*, it's likely you're somewhat aware of the challenging traits that accompany your booming confidence. The real question is whether you care. (Hint: You should.)

Others look up to you. They pay close attention to your words. Whether you seek them out or not, you often find yourself in leadership roles. You frequently find yourself at the forefront of crucial decisions, occupying positions of significant influence while having a remarkable capacity for action. There's often an assumption or expectation that you will lead, especially in moments of critical need.

For a *Type I*, the spirit of narcissism looms. I actually like to humorously refer to myself as a "narcissistic extrovert." (Yes, I coined the term. Feel free to use it.) The truth is, I'm not exactly an extrovert...unless, of course, the spotlight is on me. When I'm the center of attention, I burst forth like a Jack-in-the-Box clown toy, full of enthusiasm and energy. Otherwise, I'm more inclined to seek solace in a quiet corner or make a swift exit.

A *Type I* doesn't neatly fit into the extrovert or introvert box. Their enthusiasm and passion often overflow, sometimes inadvertently overshadowing the opinions, thoughts, and ideas of others. Welcome to the *Type I* universe.

INTENSE.

Every day has to matter. You get it, right? People describe you with A-words like ambitious .... aggressive ... and ... sometimes another a-word I won't say. The truth is, they don't understand. There's a burning in your bones that drives you. You wish you could get away from it, but you can't.

I work full time at a fairly large church which means things are always complex. If you're not a church person, think number two or vice president in an organization. My schedule is filled with meetings, phone calls, slack messages, and more meetings. Did I mention meetings? I am also deeply engaged in a consulting venture where I have the privilege of partnering with amazing nonprofits to help them better define and work on their vision, values, mission, and strategy. I am intense, driven, passionate, and... annoying. But it's not because I don't want to relax. It's just that I can't help but think of the mission, the purpose, and the potential of life. It's that intense feeling that drives me to the next project, the next goal, or the next task.

If it doesn't matter, why do it? Right?

Type I's have this almost crippling feeling that we are living on borrowed time. We have no time to waste. So everything we do, we do with extreme intentionality. This can make us seem insensitive or uncaring. But trust me, we do care. We just can't slow down long enough to show it

However, in the midst of all of that *Type I* activity, I still struggle with the 4am mental and emotional wrestling match. I call it that because the brain brawl always seems to jar me wide awake in the middle of the night. It typically involves a couple of hours of mental grappling while the rest of the world (including my wife) sleeps, as I work through everything that is overwhelming my brain.

In those moments when I question why I'm engaging in all of these pursuits. I sometimes dream of quitting it all and just getting a job mowing golf fairways. I imagine the pure joy of every day simply consisting of driving a ridiculously large riding mower at the local golf course. In my fantasy, I am wearing headphones, listening to my favorite podcast and music playlist while cutting perfect lines back and forth on lush green fairways. I want this to be my life so bad.

But I know I can't. I actually know I shouldn't.

I know there are stellar individuals out there doing an incredible job mowing fairways everyday. But no one wants me on that mower. I'd be the most dissatisfied person in the world.

The monotony of that task would suck the oxygen out of my life. Actually, by the second day, I would be initiating new and innovative ways to mow more efficiently. My *Type I* would just spill out on everyone and everything. I would either be loved or fired by the end of the first week.

Many of us have our own version of "mowing the fairways." We dream about doing things we believe would release all of the pressure from our lives. It's tempting because it feels like it would provide an escape from all the pressure and expectations. This yearning for escape pulls at us even as we revel in the intensity that comprises our day-to-day activities. It's a constant struggle based on the intense style of life and leadership that make up a typical *Type I's* days.

IDEALISTIC.

When I get excited, I turn into a firehose. My words fly like water, spraying anyone close enough to listen. I'm not sure if I'm convincing anyone or even making sense, but it doesn't really matter. I'm passionate, and that's what counts.

You see, a *Type I's* passion is bigger than life itself. It oozes out of every pore and infects everyone in their orbit. We can't contain it. We can't control it. And, honestly, we don't want to. We love life. We love adventure. We love learning, teaching, doing, going, and failing forward.

We believe the impossible is possible. We are the dreamers, the movers, and the shakers. We are the ones standing on the top of the mountain, shouting to the world, "Come and see what we see!"

In our passion, there is a dangerous beauty that leaves those around us awestruck, baffled, and occasionally bruised. We don't mean to hurt people, but we do because we are *Type I's*. That's not an excuse; it's simply an explanation.

I want to change every environment I walk into. I can't help it. I see how things can be better. At least how I think they can be better. As much as I try not to insert myself, it just happens.

Recently I was in a fast food restaurant you would know and by the end of the meal, I was deep in a conversation with the young manager giving input and tweaks to the dining experience. I just can't help myself. For the record, the young leader of burger flippers mostly just stared at me and nodded. Either he was too nice or my intensity was too much to allow him to walk away, but I'm pretty sure he didn't really embrace my suggestions.

I'm really not looking to become everyone's mentor. I just think I see things in them they don't see, the best version of themselves. At times, they ask me for my perspective. Other times, the coaching session is completely unsolicited. Either way, I still lean in. It's a *Type I* thing.

You understand, right? If you're married to a *Type I*, maybe this helps you to get them. *Type I's* are just not okay with accepting things the way they are. You know you are a *Type I* if you resonate with Steve Jobs's quote, "The people who are crazy enough to think they can change the world are the ones who do." High capacity *Type I's* see the world as it can be and aren't afraid to take the risks and steps to make it so.

INSTIGATOR.

You've been to a concert, right? You know that one guy or girl screaming the lyrics to every song, jumping up and down like a maniac. That's a *Type I*, but at the office, in meetings, or even on Zoom calls.

We are not afraid to make a scene, draw attention to ourselves, or ask tough questions. We may be intense, but we are not scared. Our confidence often gets misinterpreted as arrogance. We're not sorry for it. We believe in ourselves, our ideas, and our ability to lead change. So we'll be loud, and figure you'll just have to deal with it.

I'm always the one interrupting in meetings, always the one speaking up when everyone else is silent. Friends and colleagues have said that I have the unique ability to say the things everyone else is thinking but is too afraid to say. I don't see it as unique. I see it as necessary. We can't afford to tiptoe around important issues. We have to address them head-on. And if that means being loud, so be it. That's a *Type I* mentality.

We know that words are powerful. But oftentimes, our language creates a culture that others find uncomfortable. Your passion for improvement clouds your view and clogs your filter resulting in others being offended, even when the offense is unintended and unfortunate.

INTENTIONAL.

Purpose matters to you. You have daily plans. Weekly plans. Monthly plans. Even yearly plans. You're calculating. Everything you do has to have a purpose because you are wired to believe that you play a significant role in the world around you.

We are not afraid of failure. Failure is simply a stepping stone on the path to success. We embrace risk because we know that without it, there can be no reward. We are willing to take big risks because we believe in our abilities and our vision. We are not content to play it safe. We want to push the envelope, break new ground, and change the world.

Others happily float through life, content with the status quo. It sounds nice, but you don't get it. Again, it's like a "mowing the fairway" existence for you. It would be a nice break, but ultimately that drive inside of you to make an impact, change things, and leave the world around you a bit better is too strong to ignore. Of course, there's a dark and a bright side to this deep sense of purpose and intentionality. But we'll get to that conversation later.

INVENTIVE.

As a *Type I*, you look at the world through rebel-colored glasses of innovation and possibility. The mere mention of the phrase, "because that's how it's always been done," sends shivers down your spine. Instead, you see every situation and every resource as an opportunity to create something entirely new. Taking a risk scares others, but as a *Type I*, you not only embrace it, you welcome it. Risk-taking is not just a concept to you; it's a way of life. While others may shy away from uncertainty, you welcome it with open arms, seeing it as a chance to push boundaries and explore uncharted territory.

The allure of new opportunities is irresistible to you. Your inventive spirit combined with your willingness to embrace ambiguity makes it difficult for you to turn down any chance to innovate and explore new paths, which means you can also tend to be…

IMPULSIVE.

Because *Type I's* tend to live their lives at a quicker pace than most, they often find themselves making decisions more swiftly than others. An aversion to boredom drives us to move through life with vitality and determination, always eager to embrace new challenges and opportunities with enthusiasm. This rapid life pace extends to their thoughts, speech, and actions, as *Type I's* navigate through life with a sense of extreme urgency.

However, this quick-thinking tendency can sometimes lead to decisions being made without sufficient consideration or forethought. While *Type I* personalities are driven by a desire to make progress and effect change, their impulsive nature may inadvertently cause offense or misunderstanding, particularly when it comes to their interactions with other people. Even with good intentions, their rapid pace of life may overshadow the true need for greater sensitivity and careful deliberation, especially in our interactions with others.

IMPERFECT.

Life can get messy, especially for impulsive individuals like myself. Sometimes, when I speak at the church I serve, I receive feedback that I interpret as a compliment. It usually goes something like this, "I appreciate your talks because it's evident you're not perfect." Um, thank you? But the truth is, my days (and my brain) tend to be a bit chaotic, and more often than not, I'm the one responsible for the mess.

If you're a *Type I* personality, I imagine you can relate to the internal and external messiness that I described. Even if you're not a *Type I*, chances are you've had to clean up a mess or two in your life.

THE TYPE I FOLLOWER

With all of those characteristics, you might be surprised to learn that there's still one more. In fact, it's the main topic of our conversation, the elephant in the room, or perhaps I should say the elephant in the auditorium, worship center, or sanctuary. The truth is, *Type I's* often find it challenging to follow Jesus.

> THE TRUTH IS, TYPE I 'S OFTEN
> FIND IT CHALLENGING TO FOLLOW JESUS.

The issue isn't Jesus himself; it's us, or should I say, me.

As a *Type I*, you've likely spent most of your life in leadership roles. You naturally gravitate towards the driver's seat, and when you don't, others put you there. You might see Jesus standing on the side of the road as you speed through life. You pull over and say, "Hey! Get in!" Jesus smiles and gestures for you to move over to the passenger seat. He'd like to drive. Nervously, you slide over, unsure about all of this and ready to take back the wheel at any moment.

You understand that following Jesus makes sense, but following isn't really your forte. In fact, there are a few other things typical Christians do that aren't really your thing either. We're not exactly sure why these things became "typical," but they've become the expectations. Here are a few of those expectations:

- Christians are supposed to color within the lines. You don't color within the lines. In fact, what lines? You don't even see lines!
- Christians follow the rules. You see rules as mere suggestions.
- Christians spend a lot of monk-like time. They enjoy sitting in silence, contemplating the theological essence of God – or something like that – but you were made to act, to move, to run. Sitting in silent reflection feels like punishment to you.
- Christians volunteer for stuff... as greeters ... in the parking lot ... smiling and shaking hands. Listen, there's nothing wrong with that. In fact, we need people to help create a warm, welcoming environment. But for a *Type* I, it's not that inspiring for you. You're dreaming about how you can change the world and wondering how your church can help. Contributing in basic ways is important and we should all participate. *Type I's,* this is not a hall pass to avoid pitching in. However, just because it's necessary doesn't motivate you long-term. If we're honest, often the church is great at motivating us, but struggles to actually mobilize us in significant ways.

You might have begun to wonder:

- Will I ever be able to follow Jesus the way I'm supposed to? The way others do?

OR

- Does a path exist that fits my God-given design, allowing me to flourish as a follower of Jesus?

Let me answer that right now.
There is.

Not only does that path exist, but it's imperative that you discover it because we need you. All of us who are making a courageous attempt every day to follow Jesus and somehow, some way reflect Him in the spaces God has placed us, desperately need you.

God never meant for Christianity to be one-size-fits-all. And He never intended for you to minimize yourself to fit an ideology that dominates within our churches and faith conversations today. If I'm forced to read one more faith "instruction" manual that tells me I have to focus on being more quiet and reflective as I stare at my belly button, I think I will simply tap out.

Maybe you feel the same.

That's why this conversation is for you.

Let me pause here and address the non-*Type I's*. There are a couple of key encouragements for you to process before we proceed.

1. There are hints of *Type I's* in all of us. They may not drive your behavior or even manifest themselves often, but there are definitely bits and pieces. So as you read, there will be enormous takeaways that directly apply to your life and leadership even if you approach them differently.

2. There is ground to be gained through understanding. I encourage you to lean in because although we're loud, obnoxious, ambitious, intense, and drive you crazy, we also help make the world better. We need you to understand us more. We need you to trust us a bit more. We need you even to encourage us more. So hang in there with us as we continue to navigate the challenges of our *Type I* wiring and our faith journey.

THE PATRON SAINT OF TYPE I'S

Let me introduce you to the patron saint of *Type I's*, the Apostle Peter. Peter is hard to overlook if you've spent any time in faith circles, read any or all of the New Testament, or have connected to a church in any way. As we unpack being a *Type I*, there is no better place to begin than with Peter. As one of Jesus' original disciples, his leadership played a pivotal role in the early stages of what we now call the Church. So, let's do a quick meet and greet with Peter, the quintessential *Type I*.

- Was he "I"-centric? Absolutely. He always seemed to thrust himself into the center of everything, whether invited or not.
- Intense? Without a doubt.
- Idealistic? Of course. Perhaps that's why Peter insisted that he knew better and that Jesus was wrong about His impending death. Bold, but not surprising.
- Instigator? Almost daily.
- Imperfect? Yes, indeed. We see this in Jesus calling Peter "Satan" after he insisted Jesus stop the seemingly crazy talk about being a sacrifice. Examples of Peter's imperfection abound.
- Impulsive? In just about every gospel scene featuring him, we ask, "What the heck is Peter doing?" The answer is simple: "He is simply being the 'I' God created him to be."

In Peter, we witness the full spectrum of *Type I* traits. As we delve into his life, we'll find aspects to relate to, embrace, and avoid. It's all part of being Peter.

On a personal note, engaging with the narrative of Peter's life often feels like gazing into a very large mirror. Like Peter, I constantly require lots of grace, patience, and understanding from those around me. What's truly exciting, however, is witnessing Peter's transformation. What he was when he encountered Jesus was not what he would become as his life intersected with the grace of God. Jesus knew what Peter could be.

He was willing to embark on that journey with him. Similarly, Jesus knows what you and I can be and is ready to embark on that same journey of transformation. As Jesus becomes a deeper part of who we are, I am confident that the healthy and helpful elements of your *Type I* personality will shine brightly, while the unhealthy tendencies will largely fade into the background.

WHERE WE'RE GOING

As a *Type I*, I've come to realize that despite my intensity, impatience, imperfections, and other "I" traits, I am fearfully and wonderfully made. I've also adopted a different perspective on God, one that I believe aligns more closely with biblical teachings than what we've been traditionally taught. However, let me be frank: the Church and Christianity have often celebrated individuals who embody the calm, loving, congenial faith of John, the beloved disciple of Jesus. Pastors often teach that John was punished by being sent into isolation on the island of Patmos. But I wonder if he didn't actually embrace, maybe even enjoy, his "quiet time." While we're encouraged to emulate John, who leaned his head on Jesus' shoulder, I find myself more drawn (and wired) to be like Peter. To me, embodying Peter's characteristics seems more in line with God's creative plan for me.

I genuinely believe that many of us have spent far too long trying to suppress our *Type I* traits in our spiritual lives, believing they should only manifest in secular contexts. We've learned to compartmentalize parts of ourselves that don't conform to others' expectations. But it's time to stop. Both the church and the world need our inner *Type I* to thrive. If we fail to integrate our *Type I* nature with our faith, we risk wasting our time, strengths, and contributions.

For those who are not *Type I's*, it may surprise you to learn how much we suppress and restrain ourselves as we try to conform and emulate Jesus. Many of us long for permission—to be our authentic selves wherever God has placed us. We yearn to fully embrace the often loud, sometimes dominant aspects of our personalities while operating within God's purpose for our lives. You have the ability to grant us that permission and freedom, to nurture and affirm our gifts. We may not always ask for it, but we will be forever grateful to receive it.

I frequently engage with church leaders who lament the shortage of high-capacity leaders within their congregations. Recently, I've come to the realization (and have begun to share with them) that even if I were to provide them with ten high-capacity,

Type I leaders tomorrow, they wouldn't know what to do with them. These *Type I's* are big thinkers, visionaries who cannot be restrained or held back. Far too often, faith communities have inadvertently stifled the *Type I* qualities in such individuals. Ironically, it's precisely these traits that the church desperately needs right now. Without inspiration, *Type I's* will seek outlets elsewhere for their God-given wiring. So, while they may be challenging to manage, they are a valuable asset to any faith community.

Type I's, you have permission to fully embrace your unique wiring. It's time to wholeheartedly embody who you are, and remember, that God has designed you with a bold and unique purpose in mind.

GOD HAS DESIGNED YOU WITH A BOLD AND UNIQUE PURPOSE IN MIND.

Over the following pages, we'll dive into Peter's remarkable journey—from his humble beginnings as a fisherman on the Sea of Galilee to the awe-inspiring moments atop the Mount of Transfiguration. We will huddle with him in the flickering flames of failure and rejoice alongside him as we witness his ultimate redemption on the same shores where his journey began.

Along the way, we'll pause to explore and embrace some of the most essential aspects of a thriving *Type I's* life and leadership. So, let's embark on this journey together, with open hearts and a willingness to discover what it truly means to follow in the footsteps of Peter. Here's a quick look at our stops along the way.

- CALLING. Your sense of calling may burn brighter within you than it does for others, yet you wrestle with aligning it with God's purpose. There's a temptation to compartmentalize your calling, failing to recognize where the divine is threaded through every aspect of your daily life. But fear not, for we'll discover that God has stellar designs for your existence, and you can boldly pursue them without reservation or restraint.

- **CLARITY.** At times, the intersection of our true identity, our perceived identity, and the opinions of others can be a foggy and perplexing crossroads. Peter experienced this firsthand. It wasn't until his initial transformative encounter with Jesus and their subsequent journey together that Simon evolved into Peter. As a *Type I* individual, it's common to lose sight and veer off course from the person God designed you to be. You can even adopt a distorted version of yourself. Embracing your authentic self, even the aspects others may find challenging is crucial for fulfilling the kingdom impact God intends for your life.

- **COURAGE.** You probably don't lack courage; in fact, as a *Type I*, you may even have an abundance of it, sometimes to the point of excess. However, the real challenge lies in finding the source of our courage in Jesus rather than relying solely on our own strength. It begins with understanding how God intends for us to wield and channel this courage, aligning it with His purposes and plans for our lives.

- **CHARACTER.** *Type I's* are undoubtedly high-capacity overachievers, which is a remarkable trait. However, there's a potential downside: our success might outpace our character development, leading to the possibility of our lives becoming a trainwreck despite our accomplishments. Through exploring how to walk in step with the inner life that Jesus modeled, we'll discover how to prioritize character growth in the private place alongside our pursuit of success in the public space which will lay all of our accomplishments onto a solid foundation of integrity and virtue.

- **CONTROL.** As a *Type I*, you're accustomed to being in control, which can make surrendering control to God a challenging concept. You might wonder how to reconcile your desire for control with the need to trust in something beyond yourself. This internal conflict prompts questions about what surrendering control looks like in practice and especially how it aligns with a *Type I* faith journey. Ultimately, embracing surrender involves confronting fears, challenging assumptions, and cultivating trust in God's guidance and wisdom.

- CONCEIT. Maintaining humility is crucial for *Type I* individuals, as pride often lurks in the background. It's essential to continually examine our motives and remain humble, acknowledging that no one or nothing is beneath us. Balancing confidence with humility is a delicate tension that involves recognizing our strengths and capabilities without letting them feed into prideful attitudes. Cultivating a humble spirit involves practicing self-awareness, being candid about our limitations, and valuing others' perspectives and contributions. By embracing humility, a *Type I* can counteract the harmful effects of pride and foster healthier relationships and interactions.

- COWARDICE. Peter's journey illustrates the complexity of facing fear while maintaining convictions. Despite his future leadership role, his denial of Jesus remains a critical turning point in his life. Peter was convinced he would never bend to pressure or fear, yet we learn our fears can rest below the surface. When our core beliefs are tested, it is easy to find ourselves shrinking back. Our *Type I* life journey will be filled with risky, leadership moments that will require resilience and faith. It's in these moments of facing fear head-on that our true character and commitment to our beliefs are revealed.

- COMEBACK. *Type I's* often perceive situations in black-and-white terms, which can lead us to view failure as an ultimate defeat. However, Jesus teaches us that failure is not the end; instead, it serves as fertile ground for growth and transformation. By learning from our mistakes and allowing them to shape us, we can emerge stronger and more resilient, embracing our individuality as we strive for growth and redemption. So how do we make our way back from the depths of failure while still embracing the fullness of our God-given uniqueness?

- **CONCLUSION.** Our knowledge of the *Type I* life experience can either lead us to a darker place or a more effective place. If we cumulatively take the lessons learned, collaborate together, and submit fully to God's transformative power, we can develop a life rhythm of following Christ and guiding others toward making a greater impact within the church and the world. As grace-filled change, transformation, and self-awareness take hold of us, how can we then fully leverage our capacity to galvanize and lead in the specific context God has placed us?

TYPE I. IT'S NOT JUST ANOTHER PERSONALITY TYPE. IT'S A WAY OF LIFE. IT'S A MINDSET. IT'S A CALLING. IT'S WHO YOU ARE, WHO I AM, AND WHO WE WERE MEANT TO BE.

So there you have it—Type I it not just another personality type. It's a way of life. A mindset. A calling. It's who you are, who I am, and who we were meant to be.

I hope this book serves as a guide for you as you navigate the challenges and opportunities of being a *Type I*. I hope it helps you embrace your strengths, confront your weaknesses, and live your life to the fullest. I hope that our time together on these pages will challenge you, change you, and give you the confidence to believe that there is both a place AND an urgent need for what you can contribute. I hope it gives you the permission to be loud and large, to live and lead with passion and purpose, and to make a real difference in the world.

So go ahead. Be loud. Be large. Be unapologetically yourself. The world needs more *Type I's*. And it needs you.

Ready?
Let's Go!

CHAPTER 1

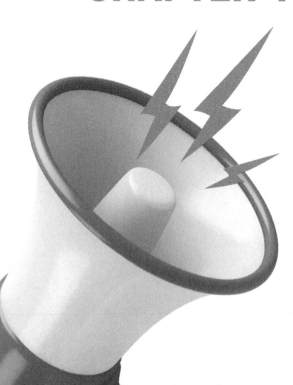

CALLING: SHALLOW WATERS

. . . .

I just wanted to steal a few moments of peace and quiet on a cooler-than-normal June morning. Keep in mind that I live in Las Vegas, and it is hot in June. No, you don't understand. You think you do, but unless you live here, you don't. Yeah, yeah, "But it's a dry heat." It's dry like living in a furnace.

Since this specific morning was relatively cool, I slipped outside with my morning java and folded my body into one of the cute Adirondack chairs we'd gotten a stellar deal on from Sam's Club. Just a few moments to catch my breath before heading out for my normal Sunday church duties.

And that's when I almost died.

Ok. That might be an exaggeration. But I did say "almost."

I'm sitting. Innocently sipping my morning coffee. Reading a bit. Pondering a bit.

Everyone else in the house is peacefully sleeping.

The back door is slightly ajar as it always is because everyone in my family has a strange fear of being locked out of our home. I know. I said it's strange. Apparently, it's part of our genetic makeup. Colorblindness runs in some families. We were born with don't-close-the-door-because-it's-probably-locked-and-you'll-never-get-back-in-itis.

It happens quickly.

I see it out of my peripheral vision. I'm not sure what it is, but I know I just saw something.

The "something" quickly flies by me, making an aggressive left turn through the slightly ajar door into the house.

That's when *confusion* set in.

What? Was? That?

I immediately respond like most dudes would...I sit there. Just for a few minutes. After pondering my next move, I unfold my body from my chair and cautiously creep into what is now a house of horrors.

This is new territory for me, but as someone who teaches strategy for a living, I believe I can find a simple strategy to solve this unexpected interruption and return to my peaceful morning. I quickly developed a plan:

STRATEGY FOR WHEN SOMETHING FLIES INTO YOUR HOUSE

1. Open all exterior doors. Hopefully, you'll flush it out.
2. Close all interior doors. That way, you can avoid the mysterious thing making its way into those spaces.
3. Grab a weapon. In my case, a broom. Ugh. This will allow you to play "whack a something" as necessary.
4. Stalk slowly from room to room. You're hoping to sneak up on the winged intruder.

I tiptoe inside and start executing my quickly developed but seemingly flawless strategy.

Quietly, I sneak from room to room, closing the interior doors to limit access to whatever it is hiding in my house while waking my family. I'm actually feeling pretty jazzed about my strategy. Finally, I arrive at our master bedroom where my wife is sound asleep, and quietly begin pulling that door shut as well.

As crazy as this next part might sound, I promise it is absolutely true, and more terrifying than I could have imagined.

The *terrifying* part? As I finish shutting the door, I glance down and see a hairy creature stuck to my shirt, staring up at me like it wanted to take a chunk out of my face. It's the size of a fist with black wings flapping wildly. That's when fear set in.

The *true* part? Me flipping out, running in circles with

my arms flailing, wailing like a baby, slapping at this thing on my chest.

Remember my wife who is sleeping peacefully? Not anymore! Now she's also wide awake. She takes one look at me and screams, "It's a bat! It's a bat!"

Yes, the mysterious thing attached to my shirt is a bat.

And no, I don't become Batman.

I become a grown man, sounding like a scream queen in a horror movie as I hold a small kitchen broom, whacking recklessly at a terrified bat as it careens around our living room.

I will never forget feeling hunted by that bat and being haunted by confusion and fear.

YOUR CALLING

In my years of pastoral work and leadership, I've noticed that many individuals struggle to fully embrace their calling due to the same things, confusion and fear.

Calling is a very Christian word. It's not typically thrown around in the workplace or at client dinners. In fact, you may think only "professional Christians" (i.e., pastors, missionaries, nuns, and televangelists) receive a calling. Nope. I disagree. More importantly, Jesus disagrees.

CALLING APPLIES TO EVERYONE.

Calling applies to everyone.

You actually have a calling, and pursuing that calling is a significant factor in your following Jesus. As a *Type I*, your calling holds particular significance and potential, but it's not always easy to navigate.

So what is a calling?

The dictionary defines it as *"a strong inner impulse toward a particular course of action especially when accompanied by conviction of divine influence."*[1]

That's not bad. In fact, it's a very good and important perspective. Personal calling is simply feeling pulled by God to be and do something. It is accessible to everyone if they are open to discovering it.

The second dictionary definition is: *"the vocation or profession in which one customarily engages."*[2]

> SO MANY BELIEVE A CALLING IS ONLY RELATED TO ADMIRABLE ACTS OR PURSUITS. HOWEVER, YOUR CALLING CAN AND SHOULD INCLUDE YOUR PROFESSION.

That's also significant. So many believe a calling is only related to admirable acts or pursuits. However, your calling can and should include your profession. In fact, the word "vocation" originally came from the word for "voice." With that in mind, your job should come as a result of hearing God's voice calling you to it.

The philosopher Frederick Buechner famously said, *"The place God calls you to is the place where your deep gladness and the world's deep hunger meet."*[3]

That completely resonates with me and should motivate all of us. Instead of trying to listen for what can be the mysterious and hard-to-hear voice of God, you should look for something you love to do, that would fill your life with meaning, and potentially fulfill a great need in the world.

As you discover that, you can assume it is God's voice speaking to you. It sounds great, beautiful even. But, as I said, confusion and fear can get in the way and sabotage our efforts to discover and pursue our calling.

I think a story from Peter, our *Type I* prototype, can help us unravel and overcome this confusion and fear.

WHAT JESUS DOESN'T NEED

After fishing all night, Peter's nets were still empty.

I wonder if Jesus, with his divine timing, realized this was the perfect moment to invite Peter to follow Him. Leaving what you know is difficult. Perhaps a bit of the Velcro keeping him stuck in his old life had already been ripped off as Peter pulled up empty net after empty net.

It was morning and a crowd had gathered on shore to hear Jesus. Peter wasn't there to hear Jesus. I kinda doubt Peter was especially interested in going further with God than he had been forced to in his childhood. Maybe you can relate.

Peter's life consisted of early mornings out on the lake he had called home for most of his life. Fishing was the family business. If you were born into Peter's family, your calling was presumed to be fishing. Their livelihood depended on their ability to find the most productive fishing spots each day and bring a significant haul of fish back to the shore each afternoon. Many fish equaled a great day. Few fish equaled a terrible day. Too many terrible days and the family would be in trouble.

This has been one of those terrible days.

But that was about to radically change.

"One day, as Jesus was standing by the Lake of Gennesaret, the people were crowding around him and listening to the word of God" (Luke 5:1, NIV).

This was not rare. People were always crowding around Jesus, especially nonreligious people. They wanted to be near Him, to hear everything He had to say about God.

"He saw at the water's edge two boats, left there by the fishermen, who were washing their nets" (Luke 5:2, NIV).

Have you ever been around a fishing area? There is a smell. If fishermen are around, there is also often a sound. It's the sound of fishermen's language. I'm guessing all of that was true this morning on the shore of Galilee.

> **IT'S USUALLY IN OUR LOWEST MOMENTS AND WEAKEST PLACES THAT HE DOES HIS GREATEST WORK.**

The Sea of Galilee is one of the lowest spots in Israel. It's the lowest freshwater lake in the world. It became the base for Jesus' ministry. At least 18 of Jesus' 37 miracles recorded in the Bible happened around the Sea of Galilee. I find it significant that Jesus picked the lowest point to do the bulk of His ministry because that's what He often does in our lives. It's usually in our lowest moments and weakest places that He does His greatest work.

Now, I realize as a high-capacity *Type I*, you may not have any low moments. You have unending success. You have so much money. Like me, you are cursed with mesmerizing good looks. You have too many amazing friends and activities. Your life may be perfect, but pay attention to those rare low moments. Jesus may just sneak in (kind of like a bat into your house) and do something special. He might even reveal your calling.

Peter was sitting in his boat during a low moment. He wasn't pursuing Jesus, but Jesus was about to pursue him. (By the way, He is pursuing you, too.) Jesus had a bigger, better calling in mind for Peter.

As Jesus continued teaching and preaching, the crowd on the shore grew and grew. There was pushing and shoving. People were angling for a better view. Imagine people in the back struggling even to hear. Jesus needed a solution. He needed a natural PA system. And that's when He commandeered Peter's boat.

"He got into one of the boats, the one belonging to Simon, and asked him to put out a little from shore. Then he sat down and taught the people from the boat" (Luke 5:3, NIV).

Two things I want you to know.

(1) JESUS DIDN'T NEED PETER'S BOAT. We later learn that Jesus could walk on water. So, if I'm Jesus, as I'm speaking, I just step back slowly towards the water. Then I take another step. Then another. When my foot hits the water, I start moonwalking. Everyone is amazed. There is shock and awe. "What's He doing?!" a woman asks. "It looks like He's walking forward, but He's actually moving backward!" another chimes in. "I can't decide if I'm more impressed with His ability to walk on water or with His moonwalking skills!" proclaims a third.

Remember I'm a *Type I* so I would have just taught standing on the water about ten feet offshore, there on the lake like Criss Angel out on a pool doing one of his tricky illusions minus the hidden plexiglass platforms he's standing on. (Sorry to kill the magic, but just google, "How does Criss Angel walk on water," and you'll see.)

My point is that Jesus didn't need Peter's boat. He could have accomplished what He needed without the boat. He didn't *need* Peter's boat. He wanted Peter's boat. And He ultimately wanted Peter. Of all the ways Jesus could have taught the crowd, He knew that leveraging Peter's boat would be a win/win scenario.

We often feel like God doesn't really need the "boats" in our lives. "Boats" are those parts of us we're proud of - our assets, resources, skill sets, and abilities. You may be tempted to think, *Jesus, you don't need me. You don't need anything I have. I don't have anything to offer of any significance.* Or perhaps you look at your life circumstances and think, *My boat is too small and too dirty. My boat is a mess. Jesus, don't waste your time with me.*

You are right. Jesus doesn't *NEED* your boat, but He *WANTS* it. Of all the ways Jesus could impact the world, He thinks one of the best is by using you - your life, your gifts, and your stuff.

OF ALL THE WAYS JESUS COULD IMPACT THE WORLD, HE THINKS ONE OF THE BEST IS BY USING YOU - YOUR LIFE, YOUR GIFTS, AND YOUR STUFF.

Peter's boat was the most important thing in his life. It was his business, his source of income, and where he felt the most valued and accomplished. Allowing a stranger to step into it must have felt like an unwelcome intrusion, especially for a *Type I.*

Can I ask: Will you let Jesus step into what's most important to you? If that kind of willingness is necessary to live out your calling, are you willing?

Where might Jesus want to step into your life? Your marriage? Finances? Career?

> ### EVERYTHING PETER HAD AND EVERYTHING WE HAVE ULTIMATELY BELONG TO GOD. IT'S ALL HIS.

(2) JESUS DIDN'T NEED TO ASK PERMISSION. You don't need to ask permission when you own something, right? Assume I loan you my car for a few days because we're good friends and then I'm over at your house. My car is parked in your driveway. It's my car, but it's sitting at your house. I don't need your permission to drive off in my car. It's mine. It's always been mine even when you are driving it.

Everything Peter had and everything we have ultimately belong to God. It's all His. He has ownership rights to all of it. His stuff is *parked* in our lives.

Yet, Jesus always asks for permission. It is part of God's character. He offers Himself, but then patiently waits for us to agree and invite Him into the spaces our lives occupy. He says, *"I stand at the door and knock. If you hear my voice and open the door, I will come in" (Revelation 3:20, NLT).*

Peter had to be willing to surrender his boat to Jesus' use. The same is true for you. Your calling is defined by your obedience. Are you willing to let Jesus in the boat? To put out a little from shore? You may have just come to the shore. Why go back out? The shore might be really comfortable, familiar, and predictable. But to follow Jesus and experience your calling, you have to obey.

When Peter said yes, he must have thought, "OK, fine. I'll let this rabbi in my boat. I'll push out from shore and let Him use my boat as a platform for an hour or so. I'll do it because it's not a big deal, just a slight inconvenience."

He. Had. No. Idea.

Saying yes to this small request led him to spend the next three years, alongside this revolutionary teacher and miracle worker. He couldn't know that because he was willing to push out away from the shore, he would see the deaf made to hear, blind eyes opened, and the dead raised. He couldn't have known this was the first step in a journey that would result in him becoming the leader of Jesus' revolution of love that would turn the world upside down.

May I also suggest that You. Have. No. Idea. You can't imagine what God wants to do in your life if you will just release your boat and push out from the shore. That's the problem, isn't it? You don't know. Because if you knew what it could lead to, you would say yes. It might be a nervous, intimidating, yes, but it would be a yes. But you don't know. And because it's not completely clear, all you can do is start from a place of obedience.

LET DOWN THE NETS

Throughout these pages, I'll be making several confessions. (I don't consider my reaction to an insane terrorist bat intruder, a confession. I guarantee you would have become a bit hysterical too.) So here's my first confession. I am a horrible swimmer. I'm a better bat fighter than a swimmer. If I go to your backyard pool, I'll be the guy sitting on the steps, water up to my ankles. I've told my wife, "Babe, if we're ever on a cruise and the boat goes down, just save yourself. No really. It's fine. Find a board like Rose did, plop yourself on it, and release me to sink into the depths. It's ok. You can let go."

While I especially dislike deep water, the truth is that I dislike any depth. Just wait until we discuss courage in a few chapters. You'll understand how scared I am.

So, Peter let Jesus in the boat and pushed out a little from the shore. He threw the anchor down and sat while Jesus taught. He casually paid attention, while hearing Jesus say radical things like, "Turn the other cheek. Blessed are the persecuted. The kingdom of God is here." That is interesting, for sure, but Peter was still in a dark place based on the morning's fishing excursion.

Finally, Jesus finishes teaching. But instead of simply saying, "Thanks for letting me use your boat. Let's go back to the shore," He says, "Let's go fishing." *"When He had finished speaking, He said to Simon, "Put out into deep water, and let down the nets for a catch" (Luke 5:4, NIV).* Deep water. The "deep end" of anything is typically a scary place to find yourself.

Molly is a great friend. She is also a lawyer, sports agent, and total *Type I*. Being a *Type I* is almost a must in the intense sports world Molly is submerged in. She is a sports agent in an industry that rarely has and barely values females representing elite, professional athletes. However, that doesn't deter Molly. She's fine with the deep end. Daily, Molly is forced to assert herself, wear confidence as a name tag, and not allow anyone to disregard her. She's *Type I* intense. Being Peter is Molly's everyday assignment.

Recently, Molly texted me and asked if we could meet up. Over a sugary, iced Dutch's Bros coffee, she shared that she was considering tapping out. The stress and grind of the sports rep world were wearing her down, and she felt like perhaps her calling was shifting. Her deeper engagement with her faith had accelerated alongside her engagement with her church community.

"Is it possible," Molly asked, "that I'm supposed to end this part of my life because God is calling me into a new season?" Here is Molly, growing in her faith and as a result, questioning her career choice. Why? Because she desperately wants to follow Jesus fully and have as much influence for Him as she can. She wonders if she can actually do that in her current career.

THERE ARE MOMENTS WHERE THE CONTEXT OF OUR
CALLING PIVOTS EVEN AS OUR CALLING DEEPENS.

••••••••

THERE ARE SEASONS WHEN OUR CALLING COMES INTO
QUESTION AND WE LEGITIMATELY MUST CONSIDER A PIVOT.

A couple of necessary comments here. First, there are moments where the context of our calling pivots even as our calling deepens. In other words, how we approach our calling changes, but our calling remains anchored. Second, there are seasons when our calling comes into question and we legitimately must consider a pivot. For *Type I's*, the intense desire for significance can make this a more frequent dilemma. Both can be true.

As we drank coffee, I offered Molly a third way. "Perhaps," I suggested, "your calling is simply being confirmed and the challenge you now face is to live it out fully in the exact context where God has placed you. Don't pivot, reset your perspective." She listened and promised to ponder the deep end that God was possibly calling her to "row" into.

Molly is a sports agent.

Jesus was a carpenter.

Peter was a fisherman.

Yet, Jesus is telling Peter where and when he should fish.

Peter was so frustrated. He was so tired. They had worked all night, dropping their nets in all the best places, but always coming up empty. When they came to shore, they spent hours cleaning the nets of random seaweed and debris they had caught, everything except fish. Then they prepped their nets for the next day. And now this rabbi Jesus says to them, "I know all that, but I want you to take me over there anyway, to the deep water. And let's drop those heavy nets where you're absolutely sure there are no fish."

Peter must have thought, *I was okay with ten feet offshore, but now you're asking me to go deeper. It's not the right place or the right time to fish. Everyone is watching. And when we don't catch any fish, everyone will be laughing. We'll come back with empty nets. It will be humiliating, and we'll have to wash them all over again.*

This is the big moment in the story. You might be tempted to blow right past it when you read it. Don't. This is the inciting incident that changed everything for Peter. If he had said, "Meh. Sorry Jesus, but no thanks," we would never have heard of Peter again. He would have gotten up the next morning, returned to the same place with his nets cleaned and boat prepped, and gone out on the water like every other day. He would have continued to fish for the rest of his life.

But that's not what he did. *"Simon answered, 'Master, we've worked hard all night and haven't caught anything. But because you say so, I will let down the nets'"* (Luke 5:5, NIV).

Peter said yes. He obeyed.

Because you say so, Jesus, I'll do it.

OUR CALLING IS DEFINED BY OBEDIENCE.

When he pushed the boat into the water, Peter thought he was loaning it to Jesus for an hour. He didn't know how his life would suddenly change. Neither do we. You and I don't know what God will do when we are willing to trust Him, release our boat, and fully step into His calling for our lives. That's what calling often is, pushing out when you don't know the result. It starts with our obedience.

Candidly, the shore is safe. The shore is predictable. The shore is comfortable. The shore is familiar. But if Peter wanted to experience the fullness of what Jesus had for his life, it required him to push away from the shore. It required him to be willing. To be obedient to Jesus' call.

Do this for me. Put the book down for just a moment.

Now, quickly Google "St. Peter's Basilica." Seriously, take a minute and check out the images. I'll wait. Amazing, right? St. Peter's Basilica is located in Vatican City, Rome, Italy, and is one of the largest churches in the world. It stands on the traditional site where Peter is believed to have been buried and was built in honor of him. It took over a century to complete the construction and its prominent features include a massive golden dome and grand façade. Many renowned architects and artists, including Michelangelo, contributed to its design and construction.

Each year, millions of visitors and pilgrims from around the world visit the basilica to pay homage and to view other sacred artifacts housed within the church. St. Peter's Basilica is one of the most important landmarks of Christianity and Western civilization.

While you're at it, you should Google "Famous Peters" and "Famous Petes." You'll see names like Peter Gabriel, Pete Rose, Pete Davidson, Peter Dinklage, Peter Jackson, Pete Sampras, and Pete Carroll. For 2,000 years, people have been naming their kids after Peter. Mind-blown.

Why the remarkable cathedral? Why all the Peters in the world? Why hasn't Peter been forgotten like almost everyone else who lived during his time? Because when Jesus said, "Let down your nets for a catch," it absolutely made no sense, and he didn't want to, but Peter did it anyway.

It's not about cathedrals and naming rights. Those things are just indicators.

He didn't know. He couldn't have known. He had no idea what hung in the balance at that moment. He saw this as just more potential for disappointment, more work. He couldn't imagine what Jesus could do with his obedience. Jesus didn't even say "Follow me." Well, not yet. It was just, "Take me fishing."

Are you in a similar place? Feeling Jesus calling you to push away from your safe and familiar shore? It doesn't make sense, yet you can't shake the invitation. You have no idea what Jesus can do with your obedience. He is calling you – today – and if you'll just trust Him, push out to the deep waters, and let down your nets, who knows what He will do with your life! Saying yes to even a small request of Jesus can produce disproportionate outcomes. While you don't know what He will do with your obedience, you also don't know what you'll miss if you say no.

WHILE YOU DON'T KNOW WHAT HE WILL DO WITH YOUR OBEDIENCE, YOU ALSO DON'T KNOW WHAT YOU'LL MISS IF YOU SAY NO.

Peter's nets were a big deal to him, the *biggest* deal. They were the tool of his trade, the source of his income, the key to his family's livelihood. In a sense, Jesus is now asking Peter to surrender all of this to Jesus. It would require Peter to let go. We love to hold on to things. To stay in control. To retain leadership. Especially us *Type I's*. We worked hard for what we have. We feel confident that we know the best way to use what is ours'. But Jesus will ask you to surrender all of it to Him. Saying yes might feel like losing. Losing control. Losing ownership. Losing influence. But here's the paradox: You surrender everything so God can leverage everything.

Years ago, in the midst of a difficult season of being a *Type I* and learning to surrender (that's a later confession I'll make in more detail in Chapter 9) and wrestling with the temptation to abandon my calling, I got a phone call. It was metaphorically my, let down your nets conversation.

It was a great friend and stellar pastor, Shane Philip. Shane started a church in Las Vegas, The Crossing, about the same time I dipped my toe into the world of church planting. On the other end of the phone, I heard Shane say, "I really want you to come serve on my team at The Crossing and help me lead this thing." The Crossing was a great and growing church in Las Vegas. I paused and thought, *This doesn't make sense. Why would I do this? I'm a leader. I'm always THE lead guy. This feels like a step back, not a step forward.*

But, I trusted Shane and loved the church, so I said a resounding YES. If nothing else, I figured it would be a reset assignment for me and I could use it as a launching point. Now seventeen years later, I am still deeply embedded and deeply indebted to The Crossing. I plan never to do anything else or be anywhere else. It's been an amazing experience having a front-row seat for the life change in thousands of people and the enormous impact the church has had on our Las Vegas community.

When I said yes, I had no idea what would transpire. But God knew my skill and gift set, including my *Type I* wiring, could be best used in ways I couldn't even imagine through the context of The Crossing. If I had chosen to be the lead pastor at another church, I might have had the slightly bigger office, the cool nameplate on the door, and the seat at the head of the leadership table, but I would not have the humbling, purposeful influence I do today with so many people, leaders, and churches.

> **YOUR CALLING REMAINS CONSTANT**
> **EVEN IF THE PLACE OR POSITION SHIFTS.**

Remember, your calling remains constant even if the place or position shifts. As a *Type* I, step into everyday confidence in your calling, while remaining open to the unique and unexpected places God may then position you. Your tendency might be to push back but trust God's plan and His bigger picture. It may even mean going ahead and "dropping your nets" when everything says it's a useless act. You just might be surprised.

But be warned. The deeper water awaits.

KEY TAKEAWAYS AND DISCUSSION STARTERS:

. . . .

1. EVERYONE HAS A CALLING: Despite the common misconception that only specific individuals receive a "calling," the truth is that everyone has a unique purpose and direction in life, guided by divine influence.

- How has the concept of "calling" been challenging for you?
- How do the expectations from society or personal experiences influence our understanding of our calling or purpose?

2. OBEDIENCE DEFINES OUR CALLING: The essence of our calling lies in our obedience to God's prompting, even when it seems inconvenient or nonsensical. Trusting God's plan and stepping out in faith can lead to unexpected and significant outcomes.

- How do you discern between God's prompting and your own desires or external influences when considering being obedient to a calling?
- How can we encourage and support each other in taking steps of faith and obedience in response to our callings, even when it seems frightening or uncertain?

3. EMBRACE SURRENDER FOR GREATER IMPACT: Surrendering control and ownership of our lives to God allows Him to leverage our abilities and resources for His purposes. While it may seem like a loss of control, surrendering to God ultimately leads to greater influence and fulfillment of our calling.

- How do you personally define surrender in the context of your faith journey?
- Can you share an experience where surrendering control to God resulted in unexpected blessings or opportunities in your life?

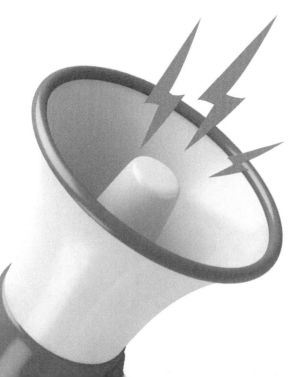

CHAPTER 2

CALLING: DEEP WATERS

. . . .

FROM FISHING TO FOLLOWING

The water is calm. Everyone is quiet. They have paused, waiting to either drop the nets as Jesus suggested or return to shore empty " netted " again. Against his better judgment and previous experience, Peter decides to humor Jesus, and he drops the nets.

"When they had done so, they caught such a large number of fish that their nets began to break. So they signaled their partners in the other boat to come and help them, and they came and filled both boats so full that they began to sink."
(Luke 5:6-7, NIV).

Notice it doesn't say, "When they had believed" or "When they had prayed about it." No. "When they had done so." Peter didn't say, "Jesus, I'm going to go hang at my favorite coffee shop, grab a matcha tea, and just think about this a bit." (Sidenote: I go back and forth on matcha. It makes me feel way cooler and gives off a total hipster vibe, but the taste is hardly worth the optics.)

No. Peter acted. He did exactly what Jesus wanted. The nets went into the water.

The result? So. Many. Fish. His empty nets were now breaking with an overflow of fish. They're shouting at their buddies, "Get over here or our boat will sink!" It must have been sheer joy and excitement. Peter won the fish lottery. Imagine it. Peter's laughing. They're all laughing. They're rolling in fish like dollar bills. The weariness of the long night of catching nothing swiftly goes away, replaced by sheer joy. Peter's initial response was to cry out, "We are rich! We won't have to work for weeks!" Immediately, Peter offered Jesus a seven-year contract, 30% ownership, and a non-compete agreement."

No, not really. But I wonder if Peter's immediate thoughts were how to find this miracle spot every time, guarantee this level of success over and over again, and make Jesus part of his crew.

But when he looks up at Jesus, he pauses because there's a wild and dangerous look on Jesus' face. He realizes Jesus was about to change everything. In that split second, Peter gets this hunch that something different is coming.

Jesus' calling is not to join Peter's fishing crew. It's not to become Peter's partner. His purpose is not to advance Peter's career, enhance his reputation, or thicken his wallet.

He realizes that Jesus is not the man who simply exists to "come into our boat and fill up our nets." Peter somehow senses Jesus is about to demand more. Suddenly fish are the furthest thing from Peter's mind. He faceplants right in front of Jesus.

"When Simon Peter saw this, he fell at Jesus' knees and said, 'Go away from me, Lord; I am a sinful man!' For he and all his companions were astonished at the catch of fish they had taken" (Luke 5:8-9, NIV).

Peter realized something bigger was going on here. Jesus was more than he realized. I think he sensed that Jesus was about to change his life. Have you ever felt that feeling? You know God is up to something, something big. You don't know what, but you sense it's coming. I imagine that's what Peter felt. He doesn't know what's coming and he's scared. Remember, confusion and fear can keep us from our calling.

CONFUSION AND FEAR CAN KEEP US FROM OUR CALLING.

We know now that Peter would become the leader of a movement. He would be the one to lead Jesus' followers after His ascension into heaven. He would be the one to stand up on the Day of Pentecost and communicate the gospel for the very first time. He would be the one to welcome Gentiles, letting them know God was for them too.

But at this moment, Peter knows none of that as he lies face down, fish flopping all around him, telling Jesus that he's too sinful to be in His presence.

"Then Jesus said to Simon, 'Don't be afraid; from now on you will fish for people'" (Luke 5:10, NIV).

Jesus looks at Peter and describes his new calling. "From now on you will fish for people." Peter did not fully understand what that meant, but he knew it was a big deal. He understood that his idea of having Jesus join him as a fishing partner was off the table. It was clear that Jesus' agenda was *not* his agenda. At that moment, Peter had to make a decision: follow Jesus or turn away. Either Peter leaves everything or Jesus leaves Peter. Those were the only options.

EITHER PETER LEAVES EVERYTHING OR JESUS LEAVES PETER.

I will admit: I'm way more comfortable with a God who fills up my boat and then leaves me alone. I'm way more comfortable with a God who comforts me than a God who confronts me.

Jesus said to Peter and He is saying to you and me: Follow me. Follow me and together we will fish for people. This was the ultimate invitation to walk away. Let go. The fish, the nets, the boat, the safety, the prospects, leave everything.

Peter must either walk away with Jesus or watch as Jesus walks away. It's Peter's choice. *"So they pulled their boats up on shore, left everything, and followed him"* (Luke 5:11, NIV).

And so it began.

CALLING DEFINED

So what does calling look like for you? It doesn't have to be churchy or require a seminary degree.

Some people, especially *Type I's*, want to do something innovative or entrepreneurial, but they struggle to see how it might fit in God's kingdom. A few weeks after our conversation, Molly texted, "I'm staying put for now. I am getting a clearer vision of my WHY for being here. I'm confident in the calling God has placed on me to represent Him even as I represent my clients, AND the fact that I'm desperately needed here." I smiled. She was embracing the deep end.

It's so easy to compartmentalize your calling and assume that whatever God is calling you to do must happen in the context of the church, most likely on Sunday mornings. That's when all the good stuff happens, right? It's easy to believe that your Monday through Friday, 9-5 (or 7 to 7), schedule is unrelated to what Jesus has for you to do.

That is not the case. When you realize that everything is spiritual and embrace a *"so whether you eat or drink or whatever you do, do it all for the glory of God" (1 Corinthians 10:31, NIV)* rule of life, your calling will become clear and contentment will rise as your cohesiveness with God energizes your life, your work, and your influence.

Calling is simply following defined by our obedience. Or, if you like math, Following + Obedience = Calling.

FOLLOWING + OBEDIENCE = CALLING.

We see that with Peter. His discovery of his calling began when he obeyed and then left everything to follow Jesus.

LEAVING COMFORT BEHIND

Comfort. I'm a fan of it. You're a fan of it. We all are. When I think of comfort, I immediately think of the "comforts of home." There's nothing like being home. If you travel for a living, you know. If you spend too many nights in hotels, you know. It can seem glamorous, but for those who do it regularly, it quickly stops being amazing. It's a pain.

As a leadership coach and consultant, I travel regularly. I look forward to coming home. When I'm returning from a long trip and see the lights of Vegas off in the distance, it is more than just relief. It is that inner feeling of rest that says, "I'm home." Because at home, I have "my comfort spot." Maybe you have them as well.

Whether you have a family, live with roommates, or live alone, you probably have YOUR SPOT. It's where you plop your tired self down, place your favorite beverage, and prop up your feet. Home is where you are most comfortable. That's great, but you should know that comfort is <u>not</u> God's primary objective for your life. Let that just sit there for a moment.

COMFORT IS <u>NOT</u> GOD'S PRIMARY OBJECTIVE FOR YOUR LIFE.

We get confused because we think God is all about our comfort. You may have even been in a church that preached, "If you come to Jesus, you'll be comfortable. He'll take care of all your needs and problems." I have to be honest. I've been a follower of Christ for a long time, and God has never been concerned about my comfort level. Sometimes following Jesus is pretty gnarly. You may have experienced that in your own life of faith. You may try to avoid it. But a dedication to comfort will keep you from your calling.

You might be tempted to stay on the boat, tending to the nets and clinging to the fish God's given you. You might be tempted to stay comfortable. But if you just look up, I believe you'll also see

Jesus looking you in the eyes and saying, "Come. Follow me. Be obedient."

You may be wondering, *Are you telling me I have to quit my job?* No. Well, maybe. God might be calling you to step away from your occupation and go in a new direction. If He is, if that's the voice you hear, are you willing to follow? Sometimes that is the invitation.

Evan is on my team at the church I serve and I am grateful every day that he's there. But Evan never thought he'd be working on a church staff. Evan's story is interesting. His dad is Bob Carisle, yes, the Bob Carisle of *Butterfly Kisses* fame. If you've never heard the song *Butterfly Kisses*, google and listen to it. But, before you do, if you have a daughter or dad issues, grab a box of tissues. Your tear ducts are about to get a workout. The song was written for Evan's sister. And yes, I've asked Evan if it's weird to have a Grammy award-winning song written about your sister and not you. For the record, he said no. He's fine not having a song. I probably would be too.

Evan grew up in church, playing music, but his journey eventually led him behind the scenes, traveling around the world running sound for famous musicians and doing festivals. It was a lucrative life but became difficult for his family when Evan married and began having children. Evan and I connected when he started volunteering at church, running sound for our weekend worship gatherings when he was at home in Las Vegas. He was great at it. Really great. He also had an unusual demeanor for a sound engineer. He was kind. Helpful. Professional.

I quickly realized we needed Evan not to fly around the world with Britney Spears but to use his skills to advance the kingdom. I approached him and was honest: "So, hey, how would you like to give up all that money and cool travel and hanging out with rock stars to come run sound with mostly volunteer musicians for about half your annual salary?"

Actually, that *wasn't* it.

I simply talked about calling. I invited Evan to consider a pivot that would mean less money, but more freedom, family time, and using his skills to contribute to something with significant impact. I asked him to consider dropping his "nets" and following a sacred calling. His skills would not be abandoned or discarded but *elevated* as he embraced a calling that placed him in the middle of what God was doing in Las Vegas and our church.

Prayerfully he accepted that call and has never regretted it. I know that because - just to be sure - I asked him as I was writing this chapter.

Do you see it? A calling is not just for those with a pastoral gift, but also for anyone and everyone who embraces their wiring, skills, and even their *Type I* to align with God's plan for their life.

Your story may not be Evan's story. God may not be calling you AWAY from your occupation or current place, but instead is calling you to invite Jesus INTO your occupation as He did with Molly. As we're told in Colossians 3:23-24, *"Whatever you do, work at it with all your heart, as working for the Lord, not for human masters, since you know that you will receive an inheritance from the Lord as a reward. It is the Lord Christ you are serving."*

Instead of changing jobs, what if you did your job as if you were doing it for Jesus? What if you devote yourself to praying and watching for any door God might open for you to share Jesus, do good, and bring Him glory? What if you were wise and made the most of every opportunity? What might that look like? What if you leveraged your *Type I* intensity and intentionality in the place God has currently placed you? What impact might you have?

A.W. Tozer reminds us *"It is not what a man does that determines whether his work is sacred or secular; it is why he does it. The motive is everything."*[1]

I don't know the direction Jesus is calling you, but if you follow Him, He will lead you into the abundance of the fulfilling life He has for you. You may be afraid. You may look at Jesus' invitation like that black bat stuck to my chest, wings flapping and staring up at me, freaking me out. Jesus is saying to you, as he did to Peter, "Don't be afraid. Come, follow me."

Parker Palmer captures this same sense of leaning into God's specific and amazing calling in our life when he says, *"Some journeys are direct, and some are circuitous; some are heroic, and some are fearful and muddled. But every journey, honestly undertaken, stands a chance of taking us to the place God calls you to the place where your deep gladness and the world's deep hunger meet."2*

BOB IN THE BREAKROOM

Our recently revamped office breakroom has a new level of coziness and camaraderie which makes it an awesome spot throughout the day. It's become a haven for our staff to gather, share meals, and unwind during the hustle of the workday.

Not long ago, during one of my lunch breaks, I found myself drawn to the breakroom's new addition: a sleek TV mounted on the wall. As I flicked through the channels, I stumbled upon something unexpected—a channel dedicated to none other than Bob Ross.

Yes, you read that right—a Bob Ross channel.

For the uninitiated, another quick Google search will reveal the iconic Bob Ross figure, complete with his trademark afro. In the 1970s, he was a mainstay of public television screens with his soothing painting sessions. And now, thanks to the wonders of technology, hundreds of his episodes are available for viewing on a loop.

Each episode follows a familiar pattern: Bob starts with a simple landscape, often featuring a majestic mountain in the background. Then, layer by layer, he adds depth and detail—there's a tranquil stream, a little tree crafted with a small knife, a wispy cloud. It's a slow, deliberate process that culminates in unveiling a breathtaking masterpiece, accompanied by Bob's trademark smile.

As we all sat mesmerized, munching on burritos, salads, and sandwiches, I couldn't help but draw parallels between Bob's artistic process and the journey of discovering calling.

Consider Peter—a huge figure in biblical history known for his remarkable moments: preaching on Pentecost, healing a paralyzed beggar, and igniting a movement. But behind these grand achievements lie layers and layers of decisions and moments of doubt. Would he welcome Jesus into his boat? Would he venture into deep waters? Would he cast his nets despite uncertainty?

Would he forsake everything to follow Jesus?

As God starts layering together your calling, you could easily get stuck in confusion or fear. *I don't see the picture. I don't know where this is going. I'm not sure if I should get out of the boat or do what I think Jesus is calling me to do, because, well, I'm just not seeing it.* But here's the reassuring truth: while we may not see the full scope of our calling, That's okay. God does. And just like Bob Ross meticulously reveals the beauty of his paintings layer by layer, God will unveil our calling as we obediently trust and follow Him.

KEY TAKEAWAYS AND DISCUSSION STARTERS:

· · · · · · · · · · ·

1. EMBRACE THE DEEP END: Just as Peter obeyed Jesus' command to let down his nets in the deep water despite his doubts and fears, it is vital that we embrace all of our various challenges and uncertainties, trusting in God's plan even when it doesn't make sense.

- What does it look like for you personally to walk in obedience, even when you don't fully understand God's plan or the implications of His calling?

2. COMFORT IS NOT GOD'S PRIMARY OBJECTIVE: It is a necessary, but healthy realization to understand that comfort should not be the primary focus of one's life or the pursuit of one's calling. While comfort is desirable, it should not overshadow the importance of obedience to God's calling, which may require leaving behind familiarity and stepping into the unknown.

- Have you ever purposefully put yourself in an uncomfortable spot? What was that like? How willing are you to leave your comfort zone to pursue your calling even if it means sacrificing familiarity or security?

3. TRUSTING GOD'S GUIDANCE: This chapter emphasizes the importance of trusting in God's guidance, even when the path seems unclear. Just as Bob Ross meticulously layers his paintings to create a complete picture, individuals are encouraged to trust God's unfolding plan for their lives, knowing He sees the bigger picture and will reveal it gradually.

- Do you trust that God knows the full picture of your calling, even if you can't see it yet? Given God's guidance and timing, what are some ways you could cultivate patience and faith?

CHAPTER 3

CLARITY

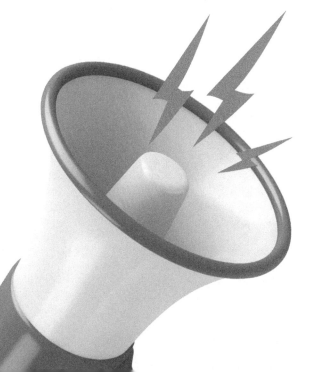

Ahh...the first day of school. While some anticipated reconnecting with friends, seeing their favorite teachers, and the excitement of another school year. I felt only sheer terror. My beloved warm summer vibe was about to be interrupted by the toxic heat of an anxiety-producing cocktail of new surroundings, new teachers, and new classmates.

I despised the first day of school. It wasn't just the large yellow buses or potentially mean librarians. I had a more personal reason.

Remember I promised I would be making some confessions in this book? Here comes one: I've lived my entire life with a false identity.

Shocking, I know. But it's true. Let me explain.

The first day of school would arrive. My classmates and I would carry our backpacks into our new classroom, where we would be imprisoned and inspired for the next nine months. We would find our assigned desks, and the teacher would begin the orientation activity I had dreaded all summer: roll call.

For most, it was a benign activity. For me, it meant exposing my true identity. It terrified me.

"Thomas Arnold." "Here."

"Michelle Beesley." "Here"

"Tammy Blake." "Here."

Oh no, here it comes.

"Stanley Co-ate."

Everyone would look around. A few in the know would giggle.

I would quickly raise my hand and say, "Lee Coate."

As if to prolong my pain, the teacher would inevitably respond, "It says here, Stanley. Who is Lee?"

Seriously? Are you kidding me?

I would proceed to explain my predicament as only a young *Type I* could, which means aggressively. I had been called Lee my entire life, but my birth certificate, school records, and official documents said, "Your name is Stanley." The teacher would adapt, and the name Stanley would fade into the background til the following year. But for the next few weeks, my friends would snicker and usually throw a few Stanleys at me on the playground.

When I moved from elementary to junior high, it got even worse. I discovered two student files were making their way through the school district - one for Stanley Coate and one for Lee Coate.

Both were me!

Good thing I knew who I was.

NAME CHANGE

I don't think little Hebrew children in the first century had summer breaks and school years as we do. And I'm not sure if the teachers took roll call. But if they did, grammar-school-aged Peter, too, would have squirmed as his name approached. Why?

Just as my name isn't Lee, Peter's name wasn't originally Peter. That change would come later, as we shall see.

Peter's given name was Simon.

Why wouldn't he have wanted the teacher to call out Simon in front of the class? At the time, names held meaning. You didn't name your child because you thought it sounded cool. Names were passed down or held deep significance. They defined you.

Peter's real name, Simon, means "shifting or wavering."[1]

Not. Cool.

Who wants to be known for wavering? No one, that's who. Yet, as we look at his life, we see that Simon was often shifty. His bombastic reactions and personality traits led to snap judgments, about faces, regrettable decisions, and quick turnarounds.

Take it from a guy named Stanley: Simon needed a name change, a new identity. Jesus quickly gave him one. Early on, Jesus sized Simon up and decided he needed to be renamed. He needed something that would reflect the trajectory Jesus saw him on. Jesus looked at him and said, *"You are Simon son of John. You will be called Cephas" (which, when translated, is Peter). (John 1:42, NIV)*

If I were Simon, my first response would be, "Who do you think you are? Second, "What is wrong with my current name?" And third, "Am I mistaken, or did you just change my name? If so, that's kinda weird."

But that *is* what Jesus did. He gave Simon a new name.

Later, Jesus would address His own identity, how He was known as both, Jesus of Nazareth, and who He truly was, Jesus the Messiah. He begins by asking for His disciples' perspective on what people were saying about His identity.

When Jesus came to the region of Caesarea Philippi, He asked His disciples, "Who do people say the Son of Man is?" They replied, "Some say John the Baptist; others say Elijah; and still others, Jeremiah or one of the prophets."

"But what about you?" he asked. "Who do you say I am?"
Simon Peter answered, "You are the Messiah, the Son of the living God" (Matthew 16:13-16, NIV).

If you were to do a "Man on the Street" Q&A with random people and ask them who Jesus is, there would be a lot of opinions, many of which would be accurate, others would be interesting. Jesus asks that question of his disciples. What are people saying about me? What is the buzz on the street?

Then Jesus makes it personal. One of the great things about Jesus is that He always makes it personal. He does the same with you and me. He wants us to decide what we believe about Him.

Jesus asked the group, "Who do you say I am?" Since a few of them had responded to the previous question, this one also seemed posed to the group. None of the twelve could answer, but there was no doubt who would first blurt out an answer. *Type I* Simon Peter *always* talks first, goes first, and jumps first.

Did you notice it said "Simon Peter"? Perhaps because he was still somewhere in between leaving his old identity as Simon and embracing his new identity as Peter.

Simon Peter names Jesus as, "the Messiah, the Son of the living God" and Jesus responds by reinforcing His renaming of Simon.

Jesus replied, "Blessed are you, Simon son of Jonah, for this was not revealed to you by flesh and blood, but by my Father in heaven. And I tell you that you are Peter, and on this rock, I will build my church, and the gates of Hades will not overcome it. I will give you the keys of the kingdom of heaven; whatever you bind on earth will be bound in heaven, and whatever you loose on earth will be loosed in heaven." (Matthew 16:17-19, NIV)

The name Peter means "rock."
I went from Stanley (not great) to Lee (not bad).
He went from Simon (not great) to Peter (wow!).
Jesus reveals Peter's true identity. Yes, Peter wavered in his past, and at times, he probably continued to waver as he embraced his new identity. But the more Peter allowed Jesus to influence his life, the more he transformed from Simon to Peter, becoming who God created him to be. He was now Peter, a rock so solid and dependable that Jesus would make him the leader of his revolution.

Finally, Peter had caught a glimpse of who he was and what that meant he could be.

IDENTITY THEFT

It's unfortunate that so many people don't truly know who they are. Their actual name may not be as confusing as mine or Peter's. They may have a birth certificate, social security card, and passport, all listing the same sequence of letters where it says "Name." They may have snapped so many selfies they can tell you which is their most photogenic side.

But they still may not know who they are. They're confused about their true identity. It's almost like they've become a victim of identity theft.

We all know that identity theft is on the rise. In fact, there's a 33% chance a person will have their identity stolen at some point.[2] But identity theft is not just something done by hackers who want to go on a crazy shopping spree using your credit cards.

The truth is:
- Your identity can get ripped away by relationships.
- Your identity can get mugged by the mirror.
- Your identity can be stolen by success.

It's also easy to allow influential people in your life to define you.

Maybe your father made you feel like you'd never amount to much. Now, regardless of the level of success you've achieved, you still feel inadequate.

You are stuck in a false identity.

Maybe your mother made you feel like a burden, and you continue to see yourself that way today.

You are stuck in a false identity.

Maybe your coach repeatedly told you that you weren't good enough. Now as an adult, you still hear their nagging voice in your mind as a constant reminder that you'll never measure up.

You are stuck in a false identity.

Too many of us have been named by others in ways that don't reflect God's perspective of us. Every day we wrestle to live out the truth while being overwhelmed by a lie.

> TOO MANY OF US HAVE BEEN NAMED BY OTHERS IN WAYS THAT DON'T REFLECT GOD'S PERSPECTIVE OF US. EVERY DAY WE WRESTLE TO LIVE OUT THE TRUTH WHILE BEING OVERWHELMED BY A LIE.

Another source of false identity is what we've done. Often, people define themselves by their worst sin—that "mistake" made years ago that still hovers over our lives like a ghost we just can't shake. Many of us receive God's grace but struggle to accept it and move forward.

Others – and this is especially true with overachieving *Type I's* – define themselves by their accomplishments. We believe *we are what we do.*

I think many *Type I's* reduce themselves to being defined by what they do. They treat themselves as doers of work and achievers of success. This is a common conversational crutch that hides a dangerous perspective. When we meet someone, immediately after exchanging name introductions, the next question normally is, "What do you do?" What we do often falsely defines who we are.

I said "we," but let's make it personal and call it "you."

Maybe close this book for a moment to stop for some honest introspection in which you ask yourself if you see yourself this way.

If so, your identity has been stolen. You've lost who you are. And if you don't know who you are, it's impossible to become who God wants you to be.

> AND IF YOU DON'T KNOW WHO YOU ARE, IT'S IMPOSSIBLE TO BECOME WHO GOD WANTS YOU TO BE.

My hope is that you will have a deep encounter with Jesus. That you clearly hear Him say, "You are _____. You will be called _____." That you will realize meeting Jesus leads to a change in who you are and who you can be. This change has nothing to do with the name on your driver's license. And, just as Jesus told Peter He was giving him the keys to the kingdom and the power to bind and loosen, He wants you to understand that with your new identity comes spiritual authority in Jesus' name.

You are now identifying and living with Christ. You may still be wondering, *Wait, but ... who am I?*

I'll let Peter tell you. He wrote this later in his life:

But you are a chosen people, a royal priesthood, a holy nation, God's special possession, that you may declare the praises of Him who called you out of darkness into his wonderful light. Once you were not a people, but now you are the people of God; once you had not received mercy, but now you have received mercy. (1 Peter 2:9-10, NIV).

I love that – all of it. But what pops for me is that you are "God's special possession." That means... Who you are is found in WHOSE you are...not in the job you do, titles you carry, family you were born into, or any success you've achieved.

WHO YOU ARE IS FOUND IN WHOSE YOU ARE...NOT IN THE JOB YOU DO, TITLES YOU CARRY, FAMILY YOU WERE BORN INTO, OR ANY SUCCESS YOU'VE ACHIEVED.

The truth is, though Peter was called away from the daily grind of his fishing business, his love for fishing did not suddenly evaporate. His identity became clearer to him and fishing became a more appropriate part of who he was, but not the core of who he was. This new reality would be challenged later as the temptation to return to his false "fishing" identity would bring him full circle. But that's for later in our conversation.

THE THREAT

But as we wrestle with living in our true identity, the whirlwind of the world around us and the natural inner drive to a *Type I* will threaten our souls. The cycle most often looks like this:

1. *Type I*'s are typically ambitious and desire to make a difference and live a significant life. This isn't a negative thing. God wires us toward meaningful lives, but unchecked ambition comes with a high price.
2. Ambition eventually drives us. As a *Type I*, it can easily throw our lives into overdrive. We lean in hard. We won't be denied. And we push hard toward what we see as possible.
3. Pushing without the proper guardrails of our deeper God-given identity will often put us on the brink. As we lose our identity in the push toward progress, exhaustion and burnout become our companions.
4.

Now ambition can be a good thing. Drive is also healthy and placed in us by our Creator, but it must be channeled in the right direction. That direction is our confidence in our God-given identity regardless of our accomplishments.

Unfortunately, too many of us deal with escape and numbing.

"My life is killing me so I've got to find a way to get out for a bit, take the edge off." An escape is never fulfilling and always leads to a deep sense of numbing.

THERE IS SOMETHING DEEP IN OUR CULTURE THAT IS ALL ABOUT DRIVE AND AMBITION, BUT TOO OFTEN WHEN WE GET WHAT WE WANT, WE REALIZE WE ARE SO DAMAGED BY WHAT IT COSTS TO ACHIEVE IT, WE CAN'T EVEN ENJOY IT.

There is something deep in our culture that is all about drive and ambition, but too often when we get what we want, we realize we are so damaged by what it costs to achieve it, we can't even enjoy it. We become burned out by trying to live up to the public pressure and expectations.

It's not so much our bodies that are under duress. It's our minds, our emotions, our relationships, and our place in the world. Ultimately, we've lost touch and clarity around our identity, providing the perfect conditions for burnout and confusion, manifesting as chronic pressure in our minds, hearts, and bodies.

Alexis Tocqueville commented on this by saying, *"He who has set his heart exclusively upon the pursuit of worldly welfare is always in a hurry for he has but a limited time at his disposal to reach, to grasp, to enjoy"*[3]

Reaching.

Grasping.

This is the culture you and I are placed in.

If you trust in the wrong thing, you are setting yourself up for failure. That's why Jeremiah said, *"Cursed is the one who trusts in man, who draws strength from mere flesh,"* (Jeremiah 17:7, NIV).

That's what happens ... especially during seasons of stress or drought in our lives. Roots start reaching to extract nourishment from wherever it can be found. But we do not possess enough in our modern culture to nurture the inner part, the private place of our modern souls. We reach and stretch while becoming more frustrated.

Jeremiah paints a devastating picture of the result, *"That person will be like a bush in the wastelands, they will not see prosperity when it comes, they will dwell in the parched places (Jeremiah 17:6, NIV)."*

There's nothing like working harder, stretching more to get, get, get, in order to present a successful public-facing perspective, and not being able to enjoy it because of who you've become in the process. You've lost your grounding. You're living a false narrative. And you've forgotten where your faith and identity lie.

I have watched the emerging generation deeply struggle with this. We have never had a generation whose identity was so closely tied to optics and so confusingly tied to outside perception as we have now. This is causing more and more paralysis as younger *Type I's* wrestle with their calling (see previous chapter) while struggling to create an acceptable exterior identity for themselves.

Too often they get stuck, are afraid to step out, and become fearful of making a fatal life error. So instead they create a false image of pseudo-purpose while continuing to search for true purpose. It's an identity crisis that limits forward motion. It's an identity crisis that paralyzes our progress. It's an identity crisis that stifles our God-given place in this world. Confidence in our identity in Christ as *Type I's* will allow us to step boldly into our calling without fear of momentary failures or insignificant challenges.

IDENTITY CRISIS

One of the greatest threats to our confidence in Christ is suffering a genuine identity crisis. Because so much of a *Type I's* existence is wrapped up in who they are, how they are perceived, and what significance they have, any shift in those things can shake a *Type I* to the core.

My friend Brian is definitely in the *Type I* Hall of Fame. A stellar two-sport athlete in high school, he attended Stanford University on a full-ride baseball scholarship. After an outstanding four years, he was drafted by the Arizona Diamondbacks and had a ten-year professional career. He bounced between the majors and minors, never able to establish himself as an everyday MLB player. Nonetheless, he was living a version of the American dream, playing America's favorite pastime.

Along the way, Brian married his high school sweetheart, and eventually, their family grew to five. With three small children and still playing primarily on a minor league salary, Brian made the difficult decision to hang up his cleats. It was time to lay down roots and start his new life.

So pause right here. If you have been the B.M.O.C (Big Man On Campus) for as long as you remember and are suddenly at home, changing diapers and polishing your resume, that can shake you. The danger for all *Type I's* is that when our identity has only been forged externally, we can become lost internally when our circumstances or situations suddenly shift.

> THE DANGER FOR ALL TYPE I'S IS THAT WHEN OUR IDENTITY HAS ONLY BEEN FORGED EXTERNALLY, WE CAN BECOME LOST INTERNALLY WHEN OUR CIRCUMSTANCES OR SITUATIONS SUDDENLY SHIFT.

The cliche (and also truth) is our ultimate identity should be found in Christ. Despite what we do or accomplish, we are who God says we are. A *Type I* can believe that fact, but will still be tempted to ask, "Yes, yes... but how do others see me as well?" Whose we are is important, but what we do is hard to shake.

I met Brian randomly at a men's conference. We were standing in the buffet line fumbling through the food choices when he introduced himself. When he did, I instantly knew that name, his name. As a baseball fan, myself, I could pinpoint his identity as a pro baseball player and immediately jumped into the conversation around the game. He gladly obliged. With his stories of major league ballparks and batting practice with Barry Bonds, I was immediately locked in. However, over the next few days as we chatted more, it also became evident that Brian was deep in an identity crisis. Walking away from baseball now felt like he had essentially walked away from being Brian.

Over coffees and rounds of golf, our conversations stretched deeper into not just the "What's next?" and the "What now?" but into the "Who am I now?" It was frightening for him on both a practical (how am I going to feed my family?) and a purposeful (what am I going to do with the rest of my life?) level. But as his faith grew in this season of uncertainty, his confidence in his Christ-given identity became clearer. This would be the anchor and guide for his post-baseball life.

When a life pivot happens, our identity and calling (see previous chapter) with God must become primary for the pivot only to be contextual, not crippling. For Brian, he began to realize the deeper nature of his faith and the role that would play as a husband, father, and human being outside of baseball. Brian 2.0.

Eventually, Brian settled into a new season as a

businessman and coach helping kids love baseball as much as he does. Of course, he also wanted them to be very good at it, and he let them know that … firmly. He's a *Type I* so you would expect nothing less.

Along the way, we bonded and found great purpose together spending a few weekends a year in Baja Mexico building homes for families in need. Of course, we wrestled with better and more efficient ways to do things, verbally tussled with each other's choices of tools, etc. That's what *Type I's* do. But I also got the privilege on one of our early trips to baptize Brian in the Pacific Ocean. A public visual of the internal faith commitment he was embracing.

WE MUST UNDERSTAND THAT OUR AUTHENTIC IDENTITY WILL BE CONSTANTLY CHALLENGED BY OUR CIRCUMSTANCES.

We must understand that our authentic identity will be constantly challenged by our circumstances. When circumstances get sideways and complicated, our fake selves will be tempted to emerge. We will be forced to take an internal inventory and ask some tough questions.

What or who do I depend on?
What identity do I rest in?
What identity do I lead from?
How am I most known by those around me?

ADOPTED

In Romans 8, the Apostle Paul leans into this idea as he writes about our identity. He starts with a clear, overarching *true identity* statement: *"For all who are led by the Spirit of God are children of God."* (Romans 1:14, NIV).

Then he makes a *false identity* statement: *"So you have not received a spirit that makes you fearful slaves." (Romans 1:15, NIV).*

Then he makes another *true identity* statement: *"Instead, you received God's Spirit when he adopted you as his own children. Now we call him, 'Abba, Father.' For his Spirit joins with our spirit to affirm that we are God's children" (Romans 1:15-16, NIV).*

Paul says that we have all been adopted. The Greek word for adoption, *huiothesia*, was a legal term that meant you have full legal standing as an heir.

Adoption was different in the first-century Roman world. The wealthy and influential would adopt in a very different way than we do today. The adoption would typically take place by a family who didn't have a son and therefore had no male heir. In those times, people didn't adopt babies or toddlers. They adopted adults. So. Strange. A family who lacked an heir would adopt an adult male who they were confident was responsible and worthy of carrying on their family name. Occasionally, a family with sons would adopt someone because they didn't trust their children to be the heir. Yikes. That's rough.

I imagine a family dinner conversation going something like this: *"Bob, meet your new brother Steward. You make us a bit crazy and we don't trust your judgment so we've decided to adopt Stew. Yes, he's 45 years old, but we're excited to have him join our family."*

Paul writes that you have been adopted by God. It's a powerful word, *huiothesia*, and Paul chose it with great intentionality.

What Peter experienced at Caesarea Philippi, Paul wants to be a similar turning point in your life, where your identity will be changed forever. He wants you to have a grace explosion as you realize that who you are is not who you were, is not based on what you've done, and will not determine what you will do in the future. You are not your worst sin or your greatest accomplishment. You are not defined by the opinion of your parents, teacher, or the school bully. Paul wanted you to clearly and confidently realize your identity and worth are solely the result of WHOSE you are.

You are adopted.

You belong to God.

You are His special possession.

When you are adopted, your past is gone, your debt wiped out, and your inheritance assured.

It gets complicated and can be difficult to embrace because so much of our daily life remains the same. You fully embrace Christ, but you still have the same job, the same address, the same struggles, and the same family. People still treat you the same way.

But you are *not* the same.

Who you are has changed because you are God's Child. His Beloved. His adopted Heir.

> WHO YOU ARE HAS CHANGED BECAUSE YOU ARE GOD'S CHILD. HIS BELOVED. HIS ADOPTED HEIR.

When you are adopted, your name changes.

Just like Peter.

And…just like me.

In May of 1967, I was born in Phoenix, Arizona in a children's home. My birth mother was a 16-year-old, high school student. So she made the difficult decision to entrust my life to someone else. A few weeks later my life was forever changed when a couple walked in with their two young daughters and said, "We want a son. We choose him."

That was the day I became Stanley Coate Jr.

First of all, let's get this out of the way. Being a "Stanley" is never awesome as a kid. If you are a "Stanley," don't be offended. I would imagine you probably agree with me. Unfortunately, there don't seem to be many star athletes or celebrities named Stanley. I guess Stanley Tucci is out there. I'm a fan of his. Probably a few others. But there's never been a Super Bowl-winning quarterback with that name. But so be it. Although I was rarely called it, I was an official "Stanley." I still internally embraced it.

With all the confusion around my name, a few people have encouraged me to legally change it to Lee. I never did. Why? Stanley is important to me because I was named after my adopted father. When he brought me into his family from the children's home, I literally took his name. Stanley Warren Coate Sr.

As someone who has lived it, I can tell you that when you are adopted, you know and feel like you are chosen. I mean, being physically born into your family is certainly cool. But when you're adopted, it's next level because your parents had a choice, and they chose you.

My parents chose me. They chose me to be theirs, bless me, make me their heir, and give me an inheritance. They embraced me, raised me, loved me, and even put up with all the *Type I* behaviors that started showing up as a teenager. I'm forever grateful for that new identity.

My adopted father died about a decade ago.

He had been in poor health for quite a while. My adopted mom had passed away a few years earlier. Over the last few years of his life, I had taken charge of his affairs making sure his rent was paid on his small apartment and the refrigerator was stocked with his favorite foods. His social security check was small, but we made it work.

For whatever reason, it mostly fell to me to wind down my dad's affairs. My sisters were very involved, but perhaps out of gratitude, I felt compelled to carry the bulk of the load. It was the least I could do. After his death, it took a few weeks to settle all of his outstanding bills and move his belongings from the tiny apartment we rented for him to spend his last few years.

When things were all finalized, I went to the bank to close his account. With all the automatic funds moving in and out after his death, we discovered that his account was overdrafted. It turns out his account was overdrawn by $499.97. So I withdrew $500 from my own account and handed five $100 bills to the teller to square it up. The teller gave me a gentle smile and then pushed three pennies across the counter.

Three pennies. I stared at them as they lay in the palm of my hand. One for me, and one for each of my sisters.

A penny is not a lot. But that represented my entire earthly inheritance.

There's only one way to get less of an inheritance: to get

nothing. But please don't feel bad for me. I fully understand that inheriting a penny would disappoint most people, but I wouldn't trade my penny for the world. Because what I received from my father was more valuable than if he had died wealthy and left me millions. My father gave me my identity. When my father adopted me, he gave me his name. That penny represented his full investment in me that never wavered. I will treasure that penny and what it represents forever.

Your heavenly Father has also given you your identity. His love for you is not based on what you do or produce. To Him, you are not your job title, salary, or accolades. You are not what you accomplish.

You are His.

He chose you.

He gave you a name.

He gave you your uniqueness - the good and the bad.

Even your *Type I*.

You are His.

KEY TAKEAWAYS AND DISCUSSION STARTERS:

. . . .

1. IDENTITY CONFUSION: Like the author, who experienced a false identity due to a mismatch between his preferred name and official records, many people are confused about who they truly are. This confusion can stem from various sources, such as family dynamics, societal expectations, or personal achievements.

- How have external influences shaped your sense of identity, positively or negatively?

2. RENAMING: Just as Jesus renamed Simon as Peter to reflect a new identity and purpose, individuals may undergo a similar transformation when they encounter Christ. Embracing a new identity in Christ involves recognizing one's true worth and potential beyond societal labels or personal failures.

- Have you ever experienced a "renaming" moment in your life, where your identity or purpose underwent a significant transformation? If so, what led to this change?

3. IDENTITY THEFT: External influences, such as relationships, self-perception, or achievements, can lead to a distorted sense of identity. Many struggle with defining themselves based on others' opinions or past mistakes, hindering their ability to fully embrace their identity in Christ.

- How can individuals guard against identity theft, ensuring that their sense of self-worth remains rooted in their identity in Christ rather than external factors?

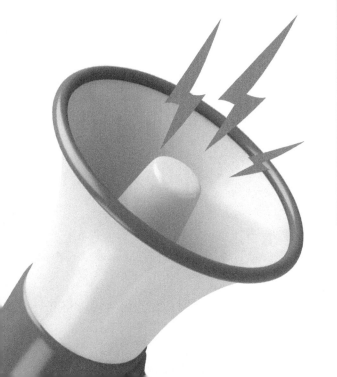

CHAPTER 4

CHARACTER

· · · · · · · · · · ·

I was just looking for something to eat and a cold beverage. The sun was going down over the water as I strolled through the marina in Everett, WA. I frequent this small naval town north of Seattle when I'm in town. But on this particular evening, I noticed something unique, a small sign that simply read: TITANIC SURVEY EXPEDITION with Ocean Gate Enterprises in small print underneath. It caught me off guard and continued to intrigue me as I made my way to the pub around the corner. Later I would learn that I had stumbled upon the headquarters of Oceangate Expeditions, makers of small, experimental submersibles (submarines for land lovers) designed to take amateur explorers on journeys to shipwrecks including the Titanic. It was a quick reminder that I want nothing to do with going miles deep into the ocean in a small sealed trash can. Remember, I don't do well with water.

Unfortunately, it was not the last time I would be aware of Ocean Gate expeditions. A few months later, on June 18th, 2023, at 8 a.m., The Titan, a small submersible belonging to Oceangate, began its descent from the Canadian research ship the Polar Prince with five passengers on board. The sub was headed to the Titanic wreck, a trip it had made fourteen times, ferrying almost 100 people on the two-hour journey to reach the ocean floor.

Ninety minutes into the journey, all communication with the crew was lost. At 3 p.m., the submarine didn't resurface at its scheduled time, and authorities were alerted. Four days later, the search crews announced that a debris field had been discovered.

The crew, including the founder of Oceangate, was determined to be lost. Experts believe the sub and its crew had experienced an instantaneous implosion deep in the ocean waters.

The investigation looked closely at the carbon fiber material used on the hull of the submersible. This material was experimental and controversial. James Cameron, the famous filmmaker of blockbusters like *Titanic* and *Avatar*, is also considered one of the experts in this field of small deep-sea submersibles. He said, *"They fail over time, each dive adds more and more microscopic damage. So, yes, they operated the sub safely at Titanic last year and the year before, but it was only a matter of time before it caught up with them."*

> ## INTEGRITY OFTEN IMPLODES WHEN SMALL, UNSEEN MICROSCOPIC ISSUES SLOWLY ERODE THE SURFACE OF OUR SOUL.

Why does this matter in our lives? Because integrity often implodes when small, unseen microscopic issues slowly erode the surface of our soul. We are often deceived by our success. The Titan was able to complete ten dives, and each time I'm sure they celebrated their success not knowing it was actually contributing to their eventual failure. As *Type I's* who love success and progress, this should grab our attention.

The journey toward leadership or life implosions always involves a gradual integrity leak. Let me clarify: Integrity is often described as doing the right thing, especially when no one is watching; living in a way that's trustworthy and honest; or having strong moral principles. That's accurate. However, I'd like to offer another aspect of integrity: Living in a way that aligns with who we truly are, so that our reflection (both in our eyes and others) and our lives match.

As leaders, we often find ourselves in personal and spiritual seasons that threaten to jeopardize our integrity. We find ourselves thrust forward in a direction that doesn't align with who we are.

You know something is off and find yourself feeling disillusioned, filled with dread, or discouraged. Learning to live our lives in conjunction with who we are takes courage and vulnerability, *especially* as leaders.

The thing about integrity is that, left to itself, it leaks, and when that happens, it threatens the very foundation of who we are, creating the real possibility of a life implosion.

The same story has been told a thousand times.

The driven overachiever goes big and is surprisingly successful super fast. Perhaps still relatively young, everyone marvels at their ability to accomplish so much so quickly. And then ... the shipwreck.

This *Type I* individual has a moral failure, a debilitating mental health crisis, a family implosion, or is accused of mistreating employees.

What happened?

I would guess that the person's ambition and achievements outpaced their character. Their influence, platform, and responsibilities expanded to an extent that it became greater than the foundation of their character could support. People close to this person probably saw cracks in their character and then the world watched as the hull of their life collapsed.

> I BELIEVE THE GREATEST FUEL TO OUR LOSS OF
> INTEGRITY IS INCREASED FRUSTRATION.

I believe the greatest fuel to our loss of integrity is increased frustration. For example, if you are frustrated with your finances, living paycheck to paycheck with debt piling up, you may be more likely to take financial shortcuts. As frustration rises, the potential for compromise also rises. Those shortcuts seem so appealing and too often, seem harmless. However, that rush to move faster and erase our feelings of frustration can create cracks in the surface of our character that eventually will lead to implosion.

Perhaps for *Type I's*, frustration with progress may be an even better example. We love progress. We love action. We love results. However, when results aren't coming fast enough or in the way we pictured, the pressure to produce begins to rise. Some of it is external. We are frustrated with our team, with our circumstances, or even with our pace. At times we're even frustrated with ourselves. In these moments of high frustration, we have greater potential to cut corners and compromise our character.

Frustration may fuel your loss of integrity, making preemptively guarding and strengthening your character an ongoing responsibility.

As *Type I* leaders, we MUST be willing to confront and process things in our lives that may eventually lead to integrity loss because when integrity is lost, influence is lessened.

WHEN INTEGRITY IS LOST, INFLUENCE IS LESSENED.

We could list dozens of examples of these personal collapses in the church, entertainment, sports, and political worlds. But the person I'm most concerned about is you. Maybe you want to grow your abilities, skills, opportunities, leadership, position, and career. But are you giving equal attention to your character? If not, if you let your pursuit of achievement outpace your character development, you are putting yourself in a precarious situation. And so, perhaps it's time for change.

MORPHING ON A MOUNTAIN

Reading the gospels, we see that Jesus was all about developing Peter's character toward his larger calling. He knew Peter would end up with enormous leadership responsibility and the essential factor in his effectiveness would NOT be Peter's raw leadership ability, but his character. The fact that Peter had his *Type I* fully operating most of the time made this an additional challenge. Reminder: *Type I's* tend to constantly be going, moving, and pounding their way through life. Time after time Jesus had to slow Peter down a bit and take him to character school. Here's one of those moments and it's both revealing and hilarious at the same time.

"After six days Jesus took Peter, James, and John with him and led them up a high mountain, where they were all alone. There He was transfigured before them. His clothes became dazzling white, whiter than anyone in the world could bleach them. And there appeared before them Elijah and Moses, who were talking with Jesus.

Peter said to Jesus, 'Rabbi, it is good for us to be here. Let us put up three shelters - one for you, one for Moses, and one for Elijah!' (He did not know what to say, they were so frightened.)

Then a cloud appeared and enveloped them, and a voice came from the cloud: 'This is my Son, whom I love. Listen to him!'

Suddenly, when they looked around, they no longer saw anyone with them except for Jesus." (Mark 9:2-7, NIV)

My wife and I recently hiked the 500-mile Camino de Santiago Trail in Spain. It was our first time so we chose the beginners' route and walked the last 115 km (about 74 miles) which is still much more than an evening stroll. It took us eight long days. Do you know what you do on a hike like that? You walk. You walk and walk and walk...and talk a little...and walk and walk...you stop and drink a cortado. (Side Note: if you don't know or haven't had a cortado, look it up. It is life-changing for coffee connoisseurs.) Post coffee stop we would walk some more... maybe eat a protein bar... and then... just keep walking. As a *Type I*, it was an incredible challenge to wake up every day with only one purpose...walk to the next city. But as the days wore on, the experience began to take on a thrill of its own.

That's probably what it was like for Jesus, Peter, and the two bros as they hiked up this "high mountain." Except when they arrived at their destination, it wasn't just dinner and another cortado waiting for them. When they got to the top, things got crazy.

They are a bit exhausted. I picture them in that well-known human "I'm out of breath" position, bent over with both hands resting on their knees. They might have internally been asking the "Why" questions. As in, "Jesus, why was this hike necessary and helpful? What are we doing here?" "Is there a point to us being breathless and sweaty?" They didn't have to wait long for the answer because suddenly Jesus was transfigured.

Transfigured—weird word, right? But it's not disfigured. That would be like a Tim Burton movie. Jesus was transfigured, so it's more like a Transformers movie, except that Jesus didn't change into a car or BattleBot.

But Jesus did change. The obscure word *transfigured* is actually where we get our English word *metamorphosis*. Jesus took a different form. He was changed, right before their eyes. The author describes Him as glowing. This mountain top moment goes next level crazy as Moses and Elijah suddenly appear. In case you need a quick reminder, both individuals are great leaders, prophets, and most likely *Type I's*. Oh, and they've also been dead for centuries.

Moses, Elijah, and Jesus are together on the mountain. It's an unbelievable, powerful, holy moment.

So, what happens next?

Well, Peter's *Type I* kicks in. A *Type I* will invariably step in where not invited or needed. It's just what we do. In the absence of movement, count on us to create it. Cue Peter. He opens his mouth and blurts out, "So, Jesus, it's a good thing I'm here because with all you important individuals showing up, we're going to need tents and, well, what if we put up one for each of you!?"

Ummmm.

Before you completely dismiss Peter, please understand that as a *Type I*, this is a normal response. If I had spent hours hiking up the mountain, and had this incredible moment with these saints appearing, you can totally bet I would have whipped out my big flip charts, grabbed some Sharpies, and started strategically planning how to leverage this moment for the greatest impact because, as any *Type I* will attest, everything can have an impact!

So why did Peter propose this, "Let's make you shelter!" idea? Here are three theories:

1. **PETER WAS SO MOTIVATED BY THE MOMENT HE WANTED TO PRESERVE AND HONOR IT.** This speaks to the way in which the Israelites in the Old Testament would build a sacred space for God to dwell. He's there fully in this moment, embracing the awe of who is present and purely wanting to do what is appropriate, no matter how inappropriate his enthusiasm might have been.

2. **IT IS ALSO POSSIBLE THAT PETER WAS MOTIVATED BY FEAR AND SELF-PRESERVATION.** His tent-building suggestion may have been a way of trying to avoid what God's presence typically meant, which was shock and awe. Perhaps he was hopeful that a tent would "keep" the power of God's presence contained a bit.

3. **PETER WASN'T THINKING ANYTHING AT ALL.** This explanation is way simpler and probably more accurate. He just went full Type I and blurted out the first stupid thought that came to mind. "Wow, this is cool. I'm gonna put up some tents for you fellas!" In fact, verse 6 might be paraphrased as "Peter was so nervous, he just started talking, but had no idea what he was saying."

The last theory may be supported by the fact that God intervenes immediately after Peter speaks, basically saying, "Hey, Peter. Shhhhh." God then goes on to clarify why they are there, by again stamping his approval on Jesus: "You are with my Son, whom I love." And then God addresses Peter: *"Stop talking and listen to Him [Jesus]."*

God was speaking directly to Peter's *Type I*. He knew Peter's tendencies (He had wired him that way) and planned to leverage these traits to transform the world. But first He had to let him know, *"Don't miss this, Peter. This is a chance for you to grow, to transform, to transfigure. You've been chosen, and there is so much ahead of you, but you're not ready quite yet. It's time to change."*

IS JESUS CHANGING BEFORE YOUR EYES?

Jesus came to earth and became fully human in every way you and I are. What's interesting is how little we honestly want to think about that part of Jesus, the human part. It's what makes Him so reachable and our relationship with Him so powerful, yet we want to shield our eyes when we see those glimpses of His humanity.

JESUS BECAME LIKE US SO WE COULD BECOME LIKE HIM.

Jesus became like us so we could become like Him. He became human to exemplify how God intended us to love, serve, be a friend, forgive, and show compassion and empathy.

When Jesus climbed to the top of the mountain with His friends, He was fully human. He was human in a way that *we* need to become fully human. His legs were probably burning from the steep climb. Perhaps He had to pause a few times to catch His breath on the way up. Is it possible He even had moments of questioning the purpose of this exhausting climb? Maybe. But then again, He was also God and had to have insight into what was about to happen. He knew what lay ahead was going to be life-changing.

Once on the mountaintop, Jesus' divinity became obvious to the group as His glory radiated from Him. Peter and the others saw Jesus for who He had always been, the Son of God.

Jesus changed right before Peter's eyes.

Jesus changing before our eyes is essential to our character formation and transformation. In 1 John 3:2, NIV, we're told, *"But we know that when Christ appears, we shall be like Him, for we shall see Him as He is."*

When I say, "Jesus changing," I don't mean that Jesus changes. He doesn't. He is the same yesterday, today, and forever (Hebrews 13:8). I mean that our perception, understanding, and experience of Jesus changes.

It's kind of like a mountain range. I have an incredible view of Mt. Charleston from my office window in Vegas. Yes, we have mountains in Las Vegas. From my vantage point, the mountains seem almost to blend together. At that distance, I lose perspective of their tremendous height and distance. While I have an impression of how massive and majestic they are, my perception is limited. However, if I were to move closer, I would begin to see the details. The mountain doesn't change, but as my proximity to the mountain increases, so does my perception. It's now obvious that what looked like big swaths of green and brown are individual trees. If I keep walking closer, I'll be able to identify the different types of trees and trails. When I arrive at the mountain up close, I can not only look at it. I can experience it and live in it.

The same is true about our relationship with Jesus. When you start your relationship with Jesus, it's like you're observing Him from a distance. You read stories, listen to other's experiences, and learn facts about Him. But as you get closer to Him, you start to really know Him. Eventually, you're so close you live in Him.

That is the key to our character transformation: living in the presence of Jesus.

THE KEY TO OUR CHARACTER TRANSFORMATION:
LIVING IN THE PRESENCE OF JESUS.

Jesus said,

"Remain in me, as I also remain in you. No branch can bear fruit by itself; it must remain in the vine. Neither can you bear fruit unless you remain in me. I am the vine; you are the branches. If you remain in me and I in you, you will bear much fruit; apart from me you can do nothing." (John 15:4-5, NIV)

Jesus invites us to live inside of Him and promises, if we maintain that kind of intimate connection with Him, we will live fruitful lives. It doesn't say that we will get everything we want or even deserve. It says we will bear fruit.

The key to our character development is a growing, vital relationship with God in which we continue to know and experience Him more and more.

> THE KEY TO OUR CHARACTER DEVELOPMENT IS A GROWING, VITAL RELATIONSHIP WITH GOD IN WHICH WE CONTINUE TO KNOW AND EXPERIENCE HIM MORE AND MORE.

ARE YOU CHANGING BEFORE JESUS' EYES?

Jesus came to be human, to show us how to be human. Jesus came to show us God so that we could be more like God.

Peter understood that this was the goal. He later wrote a few letters we have in the Bible. In one he wrote...

"His divine power has given us everything we need for a godly life through our knowledge of him who called us by his own glory and goodness. Through these he has given us his very great and precious promises, so that through them you may participate in the divine nature, having escaped the corruption in the world caused by evil desires.

For this very reason, make every effort to add to your faith goodness; and to goodness, knowledge; and to knowledge, self-control; and to self-control, perseverance; and to perseverance, godliness; and to godliness, mutual affection; and to mutual affection, love. For if you possess these qualities in increasing measure, they will keep you from being ineffective and unproductive in your knowledge of our Lord Jesus Christ. But whoever does not have them is nearsighted and blind, forgetting that they have been cleansed from their past sins." (1 Peter 1:3-9, NIV)

Did you read that? We have everything we need to live a Godly life. How? His divine power and our knowledge of Him. We get to participate in the divine nature—God lives in us, and we live in Him. And so, we should "make every effort" to grow our character. If we do, it will "keep us from being ineffective and unproductive."

You. Can. Change.

So often we feel stuck by what we've done and who we are, stuck by behaviors we can't seem to stop and weaknesses we can't easily overcome. Now *Type I's* will always struggle with acknowledging this 'stuckness', but it is real and isn't just something we can always plow through with effort and grit.

Nope.

You are *not* stuck. You *can* change—not because of the resources you have within, but because of Jesus. He is all about developing your character. He knows you have an enormous future, and your character will be essential to bear the right kind of fruit.

I mentioned my wife and I hiked the Camino de Santiago. The trail is a pilgrimage leading to the shrine of the apostle James, where it's believed his remains are buried. The idea behind hiking the trail is that it can be a journey of spiritual growth if you desire and let it be. Everyone walks the Camino for a variety of reasons. Some are just on vacation, others are looking for an escape. Still, others find themselves walking for mental or physical health. But if you are pursuing and purposeful around a deeper walk and a closer look at Jesus, it can also be found on that Camino path.

So allow me to invite you on a pilgrimage. A pilgrimage of deeper character and transformation. This invitation is to walk with and towards Jesus. Stay in step with Him. Eat a protein bar. Drink some water. Then walk some more. Do all of your life *with* Him and *in* Him. Especially as a *Type I*, we need that intentionality to keep our character and integrity healthy.

Perhaps a simple visual aid courtesy of Parker Palmer[2] will help. Think of it as a Preschoolers PowerPoint presentation. Wherever you are reading this right now, put it down (or push pause) and find a strip of paper. Any paper will do, a napkin or a scrap piece of paper just lying around. Take it and tear a 1" strip, and mark it boldly on one side so you can easily distinguish even using a colored pen or pencil (I would use a crayon personally, but that's just how I roll.)

Let the colored side of the strip represent your outer life or what we will call your PUBLIC SPACE. This area is composed of things such as IMAGE, INFLUENCE, AND IMPACT. Think of it as how we filter our hopes and dreams as we interact with the world. Type I's typically care A LOT about this space.

The white or blank side of the strip represents our inner self or what we will call our PRIVATE PLACE. Here we tend to be more reflective when talking about this place, using words like our VALUES, FEELINGS, AND FAITH.

Ultimately, we would use a deeper word, the word SOUL. The origins of our soul can best be seen through the lens of a toddler—what we see is usually what we get. Whatever is inside a toddler comes out. It is a glimpse at what the "wholeness" of the soul actually looks like.

Now hold up that strip of paper at eye level - let the strip block your view. You have now erected a WALL. This is typically how our public and private spaces evolve. We arrive in this world undivided and whole, but sooner or later, we build a wall between our inner (private) and outer (public) lives. Perhaps it's trying to protect ourselves or to deceive the people around us. In either case - we become divided.

Over time, we learn to suppress, hide, and even deny our true selves. Maybe we learn that often the world doesn't embrace those reflections of ourselves. So instead of clinging to our identity in God, we put up the wall of our public self. *Type I's* will definitely do that, especially if people frown on their unique wiring we have already discussed. It can be tempting to tuck that part of us away.

The world can seem to be a dangerous place. So we wall off the fragile parts of who we are, the beliefs we hold, and who we truly are created to be in hopes of protecting ourselves. Soon we may find that the "self" we are hiding from strangers can also become hidden from those close to us. For *Type I's* this is difficult because typically we will struggle with emotions of authenticity and transparency. The wiring that wants to exude strength and control can often find it challenging to be vulnerable. As a result, our wall can get pretty solid.

Ultimately and most dangerously, it begins to separate who we are in Christ from who we are in the world. It is confusing and compartmentalized.

IF YOU LIVE BEHIND THIS WALL LONG ENOUGH, THE TRUE SELF YOU TRIED TO HIDE FROM THE WORLD DISAPPEARS FROM YOUR OWN VIEW.

Here is the irony of the divided life: If you live behind this wall long enough, the true self you tried to hide from the world disappears from your own view. Eventually you begin to forget that the wall is there at all. You become separated from God's intention for you, who you are in Him. You become bound by who you are in the public eye.

Our culture is currently obsessed with public space—I mean OBSESSED. Everything is on display. I remember growing up in the 1970s and 80s before social media. I know some of you are baffled and confused by that. I remember privacy. I remember when it was okay when no one knew where you were.

Now, everything you do is in public. You get a coffee. Post a pic. You move. Share it on Instagram. You get a new job. Announce it on Linkedin. You start dating someone. Launch it on your stories, at the same time of course. There is no such thing as a private life anymore. Everything we do is in public.

THE CHALLENGE OF LIVING SUCH PUBLIC-FACING LIVES IS THAT IT MAKES EVERY MOMENT OF OUR LIVES COMPETITIVE.

The challenge of living such public-facing lives is that it makes every moment of our lives competitive. Because if EVERYTHING is open to the commentary of EVERYONE, we are under a lot of pressure to always make it look good.

Some of you think you're not sucked into that trap, but you are. How many of you, if you have any social media at all, have thought, *"I am going to pick a profile photo that just makes me look terrible. People can relate to that, so let me pick a photo showing my double chin."* Let's be honest. No one does that. If anything, we find a decent picture of ourselves and edit it through a series of filters until we're happy with the result. And now with AI, we can generate any image of ourselves we want the world to see.

Jesus understood this, and He had a method to combat this madness. Any time the public space heated up, He intuitively knew it threatened His character and soul, so He always retreated to a private place.

> WE ARE DESPERATE TO GAIN FOLLOWERS, YET WE SEE JESUS DESPERATE TO CREATE SPACE FROM THOSE FOLLOWING HIM.

We are desperate to gain followers, yet we see Jesus desperate to create space from those following Him.

There may be an internal yearning in us to center our lives, so maybe we respond to a sermon, a podcast, a book we read, or even a life crisis. We are determined to get our stuff together and lean into our private space. We determine we will live out these internal values and be true to ourselves.

This is where Jesus comes in. He doesn't only care about the public place. He says everything you need in the public space will be given to you if you lean into the private space.

"What if there was a place that you could go and every time you went there, you received affirmation for who you really are, strength for whatever circumstances you faced, encouragement in a time of disillusionment, and power to get through anything."[3] - Bob Sorge

The private place is where God is. And that is where you and I need to go.

This brings us to the final phase of our visual aid. Take the strip you have been holding in a circle, pull the two ends slightly apart, give one end of your paper a half twist, and then rejoin the two ends. If you did it right (okay, again, google this if you are struggling), you have just created a remarkable form called a Mobius strip.

Discovered in 1858 by German mathematician August Mobius, a Mobius strip is not found naturally anywhere in the world. If you are a fan of the Marvel universe, you might remember that Tony Stark used a Mobius strip to save the world at one point.

Now, holding the strip together with your fingers on one hand and using your finger on the other hand, trace what seems to be the outside surface of the strip. You'll realize that suddenly and seamlessly, you find yourself on what seems to be the inside of the strip. Continue to trace...

WHATEVER IS INSIDE US CONTINUALLY FLOWS OUTWARD TO HELP FORM THE WORLD GOD HAS PLACED US IN. AND WHATEVER IS OUTSIDE OF US WILL CONTINUE TO FLOW INWARD TO EITHER FORM OR DEFORM OUR PRIVATE LIVES.

We must keep saying, "What seems to be..." because the Mobius strip has no inside or outside. Its mechanics are mysterious, but its message is clear. Whatever is inside us continually flows outward to help form the world God has placed us in. And whatever is outside of us will continue to flow inward to either form *or* deform our inner or private lives.

This demands that we not separate the inner or private place in our lives. Rather, we invest deeply in it so that we will be the true reflection of Jesus to the world. The inward is "who we are," and the outward reflects "Whose we are," all working together to form our lives on the Mobius strip.

This is also a key to avoiding burnout and, more importantly, to finding ongoing wholeness in our journey of faith and life.

We all live on life's Mobius strip. There is no place to hide. Private and public blend into one another. Jesus had a private place in His life where He drew nourishment. He was obsessed with the private place. His pattern always prioritized it, especially when His public space got crowded, loud, and stressful.

I've found that my inner life is built by going to what I call the secret place. It's a place where only two things exist: quiet and God. You get alone. You get quiet. Then you allow God to fill the quietness.

I know what you're wondering: *"What do I do there? What do I say there? Do I read there? What do I read there?"*

Answer: I have no idea.

Yes, I'm a big fan of praying and reading the Bible. But I don't know what you should do in the quietness of the secret place. Yet, I do believe if you take the pilgrimage there, God will reveal it to you.

If you're a *Type I*, you may struggle with this. *Type I's* feel like they don't have time for frivolous things, and this may feel frivolous to you. It's not. You may wonder if prayer is pointless. It's not. Jesus is taking you to character school. You're being transfigured.

I mentioned how Moses would meet with God at the Tabernacle. When he walked away from that space, he had to wear a veil over his face because it glowed so brightly (see Exodus 34:29-35, NIV). In the New Testament, we read, *"And we, who with unveiled faces all reflect the Lord's glory"… (2 Corinthians 2:18, NIV).*

When Jesus was transformed on the mountain, it was His glory. But when we go to God with uncovered faces, authentically and fully ourselves, we see Him for who He is. We are exposed to His glory and transformed into His likeness.

You go to God uncovered, naked before Him.

For me, I spend most of my time trying to be fully present, with a still mind, listening as I let God talk to me.

Yep, it's a lot of … quiet.

But can you guess what that Camino pilgrimage mostly was? Quiet. My wife and I talked some, but mostly we walked, traveling together silently in each other's presence. And when we got to the end, do you want to know how I described it? The most amazing experience of my life.

You actually can do that with God.

As a *Type I*, it's easy to neglect your inner world and instead focus on what you can control and influence in the real world. That's a pilgrimage to disaster. You won't have the growing character to support what your ambition and abilities lead you to achieve. But when you prioritize your inner world by spending lots of uncovered face-to-face time with God, there's no limit to where you can go or what you can achieve. And, even better, you'll discover that your relationship with God is more fulfilling than anything you can accomplish.

KEY TAKEAWAYS AND DISCUSSION STARTERS:

· · · · · · · · · · ·

1. INTEGRITY LEAKS: Just as the experimental submersible faced an eventual implosion due to microscopic damage, our integrity can also erode over time from small, unseen issues. Success can deceive us into celebrating our achievements without realizing they contribute to our eventual failure. As *Type I* individuals who thrive on success and progress, it's essential to recognize the gradual integrity leaks that threaten the foundation of who we are.

• Have you ever experienced a situation where your integrity was compromised by seemingly insignificant issues over time? How did you handle it, and what did you learn from the experience?

2. CHARACTER DEVELOPMENT THROUGH CHALLENGES: Jesus intentionally led Peter through experiences that challenged his character and revealed his tendencies. Despite Peter's *Type I* nature, prone to constant movement and action, Jesus slowed him down to teach him important lessons about character. This highlights the significance of character development over raw leadership ability, especially for individuals with ambitious personalities like Peter.

• How do you think challenges contribute to character growth? Can you think of any specific challenges in your life that have shaped your character?

3. IMPORTANCE OF PRIVATE SPACE: Just as Jesus withdrew to a private place to connect with God, individuals are encouraged to prioritize their inner world for character formation. In a world obsessed with public image and validation, carving out time for quiet reflection and communion with God becomes crucial for maintaining integrity and authenticity. This private space serves as a sanctuary for nurturing one's soul and deepening their relationship with God.

- How do you prioritize and maintain this private space in your daily routine?
- Share any personal experiences of transformation or growth you've experienced through intimate communion with God. How has this transformation impacted different areas of your life, such as character, relationships, or achievements?

CHAPTER 5

COURAGE

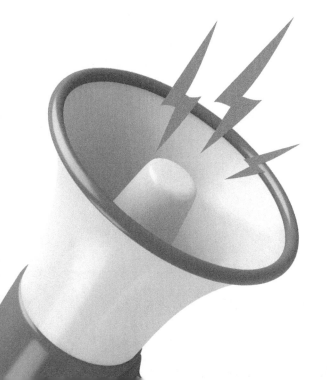

As promised, here's another confession: I never learned to swim as a kid.

Growing up in the wonder years of the 1970s, there were no floaties or cool inflatable sharks to sit on. So the 'scared of water, non-swimming, definitely not the life of the party 11-year-old me' was the one with an old tire innertube wrapped around my waist, paddling around in our backyard above-ground pool.

Did my older sisters torture me because of it? Yes.

Did it make playing Marco Polo effectively almost impossible? Yes.

Did it lead to total embarrassment if any cute girls were around? For sure.

Did I do anything about it? No. Nothing. I just didn't have the courage to confront my fear of drowning in the water and learn how to swim.

Contrast that lasting, embarrassing image with another 11-year-old, my son Austin. A few years ago, we were on vacation at a crazy, crowded water park. After spending some time in the sublime wave pool, I suddenly see him make a beeline for the steepest waterslide in the park. It had a name that reflected the level of terror the common man should feel in confronting it, Der Stuka, which literally means, "attack plane." Instead of stopping him I just followed from a distance.

When he got to the steps leading to the top that was as far as I was going. I watched as this tiny guy marched boldly up the stairs, waited patiently in a line of mostly teenagers, and then walked out alone on the platform. I was entirely prepared for him to re-think it, wise up, and tap out, making his way slowly back down the stairs. That never happened. Instead, after a brief conversation with the lifeguard, he laid down, crossed his arms, and with a slight push from the lifeguard flew down at top speed before victoriously splashing into the catch pool at the bottom. He stood up proud and confident, both arms extended in the air.

Fully inspired, I climbed the steps and took on the Der Stuka slide myself. Nope. That did not happen. Even after watching my son safely conquer the slide, I still didn't have the courage to give it a go. Plus I didn't have my cool childhood inner tube.

It was a definite confidence builder for my son. Later that day we went to the temporary tattoo stand in the park where he chose to have the word *courage* put on his bicep in Chinese characters to represent his daring act. It was a fitting mark for a very brave act.

You may not have *courage* tattooed on your arm, but if you're a *Type I*, my guess is that courage may come a little more naturally to you than it does most. I bet you have an inner storage of courage, you just need to know how to access it and where to direct it.

WIND AND WAVES AND GHOSTS. (OH MY!)

As a kid of the 70s, I also loved watching Scooby, Shaggy, and the gang load into the Mystery Machine on their way to solve another mystery. After school, with a mayo sandwich on Wonder Bread in hand (don't judge), I'd plop myself on our living room shag carpet to see how those meddling kids would face their fears, find out the ghost's identity, and solve the mystery. It wasn't until I was well into my career as a pastor that I discovered the Scooby Doo scene in the Bible.

Jesus had just fed five thousand people with a kid's Happy Meal. He told the twelve disciples to get into a boat and instructed them to row ahead to the other side of Lake Gennesaret, expecting Him to join them on the other side. After they pushed away from shore, Jesus went off by Himself to spend the night praying.

Shortly before dawn, we find the disciples still struggling to make their way across the lake, the wind and waves working against their vigorous rowing efforts. It's no joke when the wind starts blowing, especially on an enclosed body of water. The term for what they experienced is a "seiche" (pronounced "sigh-shh"). If you have observed water sloshing back and forth in a swimming pool, bathtub, or even a cup of your favorite coffee, you may have witnessed a small-scale seiche. The same phenomenon occurs on a much grander scale in a large body of water like the lake the disciples were navigating. Seiches are typically caused when strong winds and pressure push water from one end of a body of water to the other. The wind starting and stopping causes the water to rebound violently from one end of the enclosed area to the other. It can go on for hours and even days.

Cue Jesus—who, lacking a jet ski to cross the lake or an Uber conveniently nearby to transport Him around it—decides to simply walk across the water. Not AROUND the lake, ACROSS the water. (This is the point where you should probably pause and re-read that sentence. You'll be tempted to shrug it off because it's such a familiar passage. Don't. Walking on water is a thing.)

Eventually, He walks towards the disciples. As He gets close, they see Him. What happens? Exactly what would happen if you and I were seated in a boat, already fearing for our lives and some mysterious image began moving on top of the water in our direction! *They were terrified" (Matthew 14:26, NIV).*

What do they assume? The worst of course. " *'It's a ghost,' they cried out in fear." (Matthew 14:26, NIV).* Ruh-roh–RAGGY!!! Just like when Scooby and Shaggy would see a phantom spirit in a haunted mansion, I imagine the disciples hiding under a blanket or net or whatever was within arm's reach as their bodies shivered in fear. The disciples see Jesus, think He's a ghost, and begin freaking out. Pretty understandable, right?

We don't see ghosts, but there are times when we're getting pushed around by the wind and waves of life and we encounter ... something.

Something unexpected and unwanted.

Something we can't define or control.

Something that makes us question what we know or have always assumed.

There are times, however, when that scary something isn't something to be feared. Instead, it's an opportunity that could propel us into an unknown, but incredible future.

And what would God say to us when we encounter that something? Perhaps exactly what was said to the disciples in the middle of the lake.

"But Jesus immediately said to them: 'Take courage! It is I. Don't be afraid'" (Matthew 14:27, NIV).

I always hate when "Don't be afraid" comes out of Jesus' mouth. I usually want to remind Him, *"Easy for You to say."*

They were obviously afraid, appropriately afraid. But they were also at a defining moment. It was one of those forks in the road (or oar in the lake) moments where you have to decide: What kind of person am I going to be? Am I going to put what I believe into action? Or just talk about it?

ORDINARY EXTRAORDINARY

So… what kind of person do you want to be? How do you want to be known?

When your friends talk about you behind your back, when you leave work and people are still there and chat about you, or when you walk away from the sidelines of your kid's soccer game and the other parents say something about you, what would you like them to say?

I believe most people – especially *Type I's* – want to be extraordinary. You feel that, right? You believe God gave you life. That He is for you and with you. Therefore your life has meaning and is leading somewhere.

You don't want to settle for an ordinary life.Unfortunately, it's the easiest thing to do: live the same way as everyone else and do what you've always done. In fact, if you and I are not intentional, that's exactly where our lives will settle.

Why do you settle?

First, I wonder if it's because you've lost sight of who you are. Maybe you've settled for a version of yourself based on the opinions of others. You've accepted you are who they think you should be. But what if they're wrong? Spoiler: They probably are. They believe you should be normal and average, but that's not what God wants for you. God looks at you as someone He made just the way He wanted, who He has forgiven, redeemed, lives inside of, and has big plans for.

Yes, you!

This is another reason it's so important to know who and Whose you are.

He didn't create you to be extraordinary so that you could settle for less.

You may also settle because you've forgotten. Forgotten the God of your childhood. Forgotten all the times God was there for you. Forgotten the prayers He's answered. Forgotten that God promised, *"I will be with you" (Judges 6:16, NIV)* and that *"If God is for us, who can be against us?" (Romans 8:21, NIV)*. As a result, you're tempted to shrink back instead of boldly moving forward.

DISCERNMENT IS CRITICAL BECAUSE THOSE WE LOVE THE MOST CAN OFTEN LIMIT US FROM FOLLOWING THE PLAN OF THE ONE WHO LOVES US MOST.

Those around us can also impact our courage. As impulsive *Type I's*, we can be quick to act, which is why we need the wisdom of mentors. Yes, courage can look like action, but courage can also look like waiting, praying, and discerning. Discernment is critical because those we love the most can often limit us from following the plan of the One who loves us most. Suffice it to say, the right voices with a healthy understanding of who you will be are important when you step out onto the choppy waters of life.

> IT'S A LITTLE SHOCKING TO ME THAT THE SAME FOLLOWERS
> WHO SAW HIM PROVIDE A MIRACULOUS DINNER FOR THOUSANDS
> JUST A FEW HOURS EARLIER WOULD NOW BE TERRIFIED
> AND SURPRISED BY ANYTHING HE DOES

It's a little shocking to me that the same followers of Jesus who saw Him do incredible things like using a child's lunch to provide a miraculous dinner for thousands just a few hours earlier would now be terrified and surprised by ANYTHING He does.

Perhaps all of that has led you to settle, to do life the way everyone else does, to make decisions the way they do, and to have low expectations and small dreams the way they do.

But what if God opened your eyes? What if you could see yourself the way He sees you and have His vision for your life?

I believe that's what God wants to do. He longs for you to see yourself the way He does. He wants you to walk out of the ordinary and into the extraordinary. That's the life He's inviting you into.

What if you entered into a daring and divine partnership with God that led you to extraordinary? What if you woke up every morning and had the courage to ask, *How would an extraordinary person, who happens to be me, live this day? What would an extraordinary person, who happens to be me, do if they knew they had a supernatural, empowering relationship with God? What would an extraordinary person, who happens to be me, do with this day, knowing that God is in me, with me, and for me?*

It sounds exciting, but the truth is that it's not easy and will take courage – real, serious, courage. You'll need courage to be the extraordinary you and respond to life in a bigger, better, more daring way.

It may feel like that's more courage than you possess.

If so, there's good news. Unfortunately, the good news takes us back out to the water.

WATER WALKING

Jesus came walking along the choppy surface of the lake and everyone freaked out. Jesus said, *"Take courage! It is I. Don't be afraid"* (Matthew 14:27, NIV).

You hear Jesus' voice. You realize that, in addition to being able to multiply a sack lunch into an all-you-can-eat buffet, Jesus can walk on water.

What do you do at that moment?

The ordinary reaction is to be afraid.

The extraordinary reaction is, *"'Lord if it's you,' Peter replied, 'tell me to come to you on the water'"* (Matthew 14:28, NIV).

Do you think Jesus smiled? I bet His eyes lit up and He had the biggest smile ever. This is what He'd been looking for – radical, reckless trust.

Why do you think Peter asked? The wind is howling. Waves are crashing. He just got through what felt like a terrifying ghost citing. He had zero evidence that he had water-walking ability. Why did Peter propose he get out of the boat and walk to Jesus?

Well, what kind of person did Peter want to be? He could be ordinary. But he chose to be extraordinary, to do what no one but the Son of God had ever done.

Jesus' reply? *"'Come,' he said"* (Matthew 14:29, NIV).

How do you think Peter was feeling at that moment? He was probably excited, but I'm guessing he was mostly afraid. He had to be afraid, right? He had fear, but he also had courage. That's an important point: Courage is not the absence of fear; it is confidence in the presence of God.

Peter gets the go-ahead from Jesus: *"Then Peter got down out of the boat, walked on the water, and came toward Jesus"* (Matthew 14:29, NIV).

> THE CLOSER YOU WALK WITH GOD; THE
> MORE COURAGE WILL BE REQUIRED.

Can I let you in on something? The closer you walk with God; the more courage will be required. Some assume God is trying to turn bad people into good people, but I believe God is trying to turn fearful people into dangerous people. He's calling all of us to get out of the boat, to step into the unknown and fear-inducing. That demands courage. Again, the closer you walk with God; the more courage will be required.

As you walk closer to Jesus, you will require more courage, but you will also possess more courage. Because the best place to find courage is in Jesus.

That's what Peter does. He throws his leg over the side of the boat, puts his foot down on a surface not solid enough to support his weight and bam! He's walking as he locks in on Jesus' eyes.

Do you know the thrill of walking on water? Now I'm not suggesting you fill your bathtub and try to use the water as a trampoline. I'm asking: Have you ever done something you never would have done except you felt called to do it by God? Have you ever accomplished something that would have been impossible without the supernatural empowerment of God?

I'll never forget the first time my wife and I visited Las Vegas. The reason isn't what you may be thinking. We weren't hitting Vegas for a fun weekend. We came to Vegas in the middle of our first year of marriage at the invitation of a small, growing church that had expressed interest in us joining their staff team. Yes, a church in Sin City. [Sidenote: Despite its reputation, Las Vegas is much more than the 4.2 miles of lights and casinos that make up The Strip. It's a compassionate community with some of the healthiest churches in the country.] That fact may shock you, so imagine this wide-eyed, newlywed Christian couple considering making Las Vegas home. We were freaked out.

THE BEST PLACE TO FIND COURAGE IS IN JESUS.

Even so, we flew to Las Vegas from our home in Seattle to check it out. After landing at midnight and recovering from the shock of the airport being filled with slot machines, we found our way to baggage claim where we met our host of the weekend who proceeded to drive us directly up The Strip. Courageous, but potentially an unwise move. The lights, the people, all of it was … a lot. I'll never forget the strange look in my wife's eyes as she took it all in.

But guess what? After spending the weekend in Vegas, meeting people who lived there, and catching a vision of what was possible, we made the decision to make Vegas home. Over thirty years later, we continue to call Vegas home. It was a decision that required courage. Could we see God's desire, step out of the boat of our comfortable, normal life, and step into God's future in a city that we felt uniquely and mysteriously called to? With courage, we answered the call. Like Peter, that was our "walk on water" moment. It required us to lock eyes on Jesus and step courageously into the waves of the unknown. And I can't imagine life if we had stayed put.

COURAGE CONTRACTION

Peter is out of the boat, eyes locked on Jesus, doing the impossible, brimming with courage. He's living his best *Type I* life at the moment. But … *"When he saw the wind, he was afraid and, beginning to sink, cried out, 'Lord, save me!' Immediately Jesus reached out his hand and caught him. 'You of little faith,' he said, 'Why did you doubt?'"* (Matthew 14:30-31, NIV).

Wow!

What happened?

> COURAGE CAN GET US OUT OF THE BOAT, BUT
> EVENTUALLY OUR COURAGE WILL WANE.

What happened was exactly what would happen to most of us. Peter did what most of us do. Instead of looking up, he started looking around. That's when he "saw the wind" and his courage started leaking. Which is interesting. Jesus was right there in front of him, but instead of seeing Jesus, he saw the wind. I'm pretty sure wind is one thing you can't see, but Peter saw it affecting his surroundings and thought he might be unable to continue doing what he was doing very successfully.

Suddenly, his focus shifted from Jesus' supernatural ability to his own natural ability. The extraordinary thing he was doing felt tenuous, so he reverted to the ordinary. Ordinarily, people sink in water, and so did Peter.

Peter experienced what I call courage contraction. He teaches us an important lesson: Courage can get us out of the boat, but eventually our courage will wane. It's okay that we don't have sufficient store of what we need within ourselves because we are out on the waves with Jesus. If we just lock eyes with Him, we can walk on water. He gives us a level of deep, overcoming courage we don't naturally possess. Type I's may tend to take those courageous steps more often and more quickly than others, but where we focus on eyes makes all the difference. And if (or when) our gaze shifts away from Jesus, and all we see is the storm around us, we won't drown because He's always there to reach out His hand to catch us.

PROFILE IN COURAGE

We all need examples of courage to learn from and inspire us. It's probably helpful to go a little deeper than my son taking on a massive water slide. So to appropriately do that, let me first introduce you to Deborah.

We find Deborah's story in the Old Testament book of Judges, chapters four and five. For context, at that time, the people of Israel were led by judges, not politicians or kings. However, these were not courtroom judges like Judge Judy or Judge Wapner. While these leaders listened to and settled disputes, they also played a huge role in delivering the nation from various outside oppressors.

Delivering Israel was a full-time gig during this time. The nation of Israel was created by God to be so unique in how they operated and lived, that all the nations around would see it and would want to follow their God. God intended the nation to be extraordinary. He also intended them to be an example. But this would require courage as well. The rest of the world was supposed to be able to look at them and think they've got it going on. That was the point. They had a destiny. In some ways, they were to be heroic.

But when they finally got into the promised land, they did exactly what most of us do. Instead of looking up, they started looking around. They noticed other things and how other groups functioned. As they looked around at what others had, they thought, "I want what they have. Their lives look better, easier, and better." Although God tried to convince them otherwise, they wouldn't have it. They started building idols and simply being ORDINARY like all the nations around them when they were supposed to be COURAGEOUS. They were supposed to be the ones who would step out of the boat, not just sit there. And because of this lack of courage, the nation of Israel throughout the book of Judges goes through a vicious cycle.

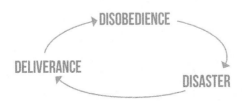

The cycle looked like this: Disobedience - Disaster - Deliverance. And this cyclical pattern played out from generation to generation. They would disobey. This disobedience and straying from God's purpose would eventually bring disaster, usually in the form of an outside enemy invading, conquering, and oppressing.

Then, they would cry out to God to forgive them and promise never to do that again, so God, in His mercy and grace, would deliver and bless them until they eventually disobeyed again. These various "judges" would be called upon to provide the leadership, direction, and God-inspired correction to bring the people back to Him, to be courageous instruments of deliverance. These judges typically had a lot of *Type I* flowing through their wiring as well.

Deborah was one of these judges. She was DEFINITELY a *Type I* and during Deborah's time "on the bench," we find that *"the Israelites did evil in the eyes of the Lord" (Judges 4:1, NIV)*. As a result, they became oppressed by the nation of Canaan and finally, after twenty years, they cried out to God for assistance. I'm not sure why it took them twenty years, but it did.

Deborah, directed by God, sends for a soldier named Barak and commands him to take ten thousand men to Mount Tabor. He and his men serve as a decoy and draw the enemy's armies with their 900 chariots to the Kishon River. Barak's response is awesome and shows his dependence on Deborah's courage. He answers, *"If you go with me, I will go; but if you don't go with me, I won't go." (Judges 4:8, NIV)*.

That's not exactly the radical independent commitment you might hope to get from a general of the army. We might call this "conditional courage". This is courage with a catch. The general's catch was he was unprepared to go forward without Deborah close by. He needed her courage and leadership to fill in the gap for the deficit he had.

Deborah sighs. The Bible doesn't say that, but I'm sure she sighed. *"'Certainly I will go with you,' said Deborah. 'But because of the course you are taking, the honor will not be yours, for the Lord will deliver Sisera into the hands of a woman.'" (Judges 4:9, NIV)*.

Deborah is the only judge who was also called a prophet. A prophet heard directly from God and was His mouthpiece to the people. She was also a wife, probably a mother as well as being a military, civic, political, and spiritual leader. I've heard her described as the President, the Pope, and Rambo all wrapped up in one. Not a bad resume for a middle-aged woman living in the hierarchical culture of the Middle East at that time. She was confident that God was going to deliver His people.

In verse 10 we read that Barak leads the army to the exact place Deborah told him. Then there seems to be a weird digression from the main story, *"Now Heber the Kenite had left the other Kenites, the descendants of Hobab, Moses' brother-in-law, and pitched his tent by the great tree in Zaanannim near Kedesh"* (Judges 4:11, NIV). A battle is about to go down, and the author seems to digress by telling us that some guy and his wife can't get along with their neighbors, so they buy an RV and park it out in the middle of the desert. Pay attention. This seemingly unimportant detail is not a random detail at all as we shall soon discover. Just hold that thought.

Deborah then directs Barak and the army down to a river basin at the base of Mt. Tabor. *"Then Deborah said to Barak, 'Go! This is the day the Lord has given Sisera into your hands. Has not the Lord gone ahead of you?' So Barak went down Mount Tabor, with ten thousand men following him. At Barak's advance, the Lord routed Sisera and all his chariots and army by the sword, and Sisera got down from his chariot and fled on foot."* (Judges 4:14-15, NIV).

Deborah had strategically led General Sisera, leader of the Canaanite army, and his men to the River Kishon for the battle. However, a huge flash flood rendered Sisera's chariots useless as they became stuck in the mud.

Sisera abandons the chariots and decides to make his getaway on foot, which is when the story takes another dramatic turn with a second woman taking a lead role. As Sisera is running for his life, he comes, *"to the tent of Jael, the wife of Heber the Kenite"* (Judges 4:17, NIV).

Remember them? They're the ones in the RV out in the middle of nowhere. But the middle of nowhere just happens to be right in the path where Sisera is attempting to escape.

"Jael went out to meet Sisera and said to him, 'Come, my lord, come right in. Don't be afraid.' So he entered her tent, and she covered him with a blanket ... But Jael, Heber's wife, picked up a tent peg and a hammer and went quietly to him while he lay fast asleep, exhausted. She drove the peg through his temple into the ground, and he died" (Judges 4:18, 21, NIV).

And she walked outside and said ... "Nailed it."

The entire peg-in-the-head thing is pretty dramatic and either exciting or revolting depending on your perspective, but it definitely gets your attention.

Here's the main thing to recognize. God delivered Israel by leveraging the courage of two women, Deborah and Jael. When courage was desperately needed, these two women stepped up.

I noticed two things we can learn from Deborah's courage and *Type I* leadership at this moment.

First, Lean into your Calling.

In Judges 5, we read Deborah's song – a worship song written after the battle to celebrate what God had done. In verse 7, she says something pretty interesting and revealing, *"Villagers in Israel would not fight; they held back until I, Deborah, arose, until I arose, a mother in Israel."*

Deborah rose up and responded to God's call to lead the people. (Remember that calling thing from back in chapter one? This is an example of that.)

Think of all the reasons why that is astonishing. Even today, people often act surprised when a woman leans in and takes the lead. While change is slow, thankfully, progress is being made as those in leadership positions make spaces and extend opportunities for the *Type I* women to lean into their God-given wiring. But back then, for a woman to step up was an almost unheard of occurrence because the society and culture did not encourage, or pave an easy path. Deborah had so many reasons she could have denied her calling, but she was bold and brave.

She overcame enormous external obstacles in the patriarchal culture in which she lived, but I bet some of her greatest hindrances were actually *internal.* Former Facebook executive Sheryl Sandberg writes about this in *Lean In,*

"Internal obstacles are rarely discussed and often underplayed. Throughout my life, I was told over and over about inequalities in the workplace and how hard it would be to have a career and a family. I rarely heard anything however about the ways I might hold myself back. These internal obstacles deserve a lot

more attention in part because they are under our control. We can dismantle the hurdles in ourselves today. We can start at this very moment."

That's why I love that Deborah calls herself a *Mother in Israel* in her post-battle reflective victory song. She chose to use that description over prophet, judge, or leader. It may not have looked as impressive on her LinkedIn page, but she wasn't trying to prove herself by reminding others of her position. Instead, Deborah leaned into who God made her to be and then simply led.

If you want to live a courageous life, you will have to overcome external obstacles and perhaps even some of the internal lies you tell yourself.

We've already talked extensively about calling. The magic happens when you go beyond simply discerning it and actually begin leaning into and living it.

You can do that.

You can lean into your calling instead of caving into others' expectations or the lies that fill you with fear. But to lean in, you'll also need to lean on someone else.

Second, Lean on God.

Sufficient courage does not come naturally, especially when it's leading troops against the armies of a more powerful nation. So where did Deborah find her courage? She drew her confidence and strength from her relationship with God.

Before she was a *warrior*, she was a *worshiper*. It was in quiet moments with God that she received direction, wisdom, and confidence.

BEFORE SHE WAS A WARRIOR, SHE WAS A WORSHIPER.

I respect that and need to learn from Deborah because I lean more toward warrior than worshiper. I like to charge in, go after, press hard, and get stuff done. My wife constantly reminds me that my tendency is to "plow through life." She's not wrong.

In fact, you can often hear me yell, "Let's Go!" down the office hallway. I want to see action happening. However, action can give a false sense of courageous progress. It's not that I don't believe in worship. I do. When I get a free moment from all my striving, conquering, and achieving, I check in with God. If you're a *Type I*, you feel me.

Not Deborah.

She knew how to lean on God as she leaned into her role and calling.

How did she know the exact day to have the Israelites go into battle? God revealed it to her. She knew how to listen to God and wait on God.

She had no doubt Who the true source of her gifts and strength was and she recognized it wasn't herself. She prioritized going to the Source. Go ahead. Read Judges chapter five, and you'll see how closely Deborah's actions are tied to her relationship with and understanding of God. They cannot be separated. Deborah lived by a game-changing math equation we need to experience: Human engagement + Heavenly intervention = Unbeatable Combination

HUMAN ENGAGEMENT + HEAVENLY INTERVENTION = UNBEATABLE COMBINATION

What is important for us to see as *Type I's* is that when we are fully engaged in what God is doing and there is supernatural, heavenly involvement... all things are possible. So this would be a great moment for you to do a self-audit. Are you lacking somewhere in this equation? Has God wanted to do something with you, but you have yet to engage? Or is it possible you are moving so hard and fast that you haven't paused and invited God to be part of that process? Either one will cause you to miss out on that unbeatable combination.

Over and over, we see Deborah knew exactly why she was successful because she gave credit to whom credit is due. So please remember this: the CLOSER you walk to God, the more COURAGE will be required!

FOR THOSE ALONGSIDE

As a *Type I*, I'm typically the first to offer innovations, ideas, and ideals. They flow naturally from me, and I can typically see how we are going to get from here to there quickly. However, sometimes my way of seeing the flow is more in leaps than steps.

In my excitement and even courageous mindset, I'm often limited in my inability to see the incremental steps to take and potholes to avoid in order to reach the desired destination. So the wise thing for me is to recognize my limitations without sacrificing my confidence. To do that, it requires surrounding myself with people whom I have empowered to overcome my limited macro view of the way forward while also allowing (even encouraging me) to live out my *Type I*, without hijacking the health and mission of my organization.

Too often, *Type I's* are unwilling to acknowledge our limitations, not only to others but also to ourselves. But when we recognize our limitations, we can overcome them and even rely on other people who are strong where we are weak. You may be one of those individuals who gladly navigates your *Type I* spouse, friend, boss, or coworker. Here are a couple of helpful perspectives from supporting characters in Deborah's story.

The two supporting characters in Deborah's story are men, Barak and Lappidoth. By the way, it's important and fascinating to note that there is no instance of a man challenging Deborah's authority or refusing to follow her lead. This plays against the stereotype that only men are *Type I's* while women are merely supporting cast. This is a truthful and needed role reversal as a subplot in this story.

This is the moment I would like to appropriately pause and state what may or may not be obvious. There is no gender filter for Type I wiring. I recognize that Peter is our chosen patron saint for this conversation, but this is an obvious choice based on the depth and detail of his Type I narrative threaded throughout the New Testament. It is not an indicator or affirmation that Type I wiring exists mainly in males and women should suppress any of these traits. On the contrary. It is a sexist stereotype that is unfortunate and should continue to be debunked. Deborah goes a long way to change this narrative, and we should aggressively continue that trend. So...

Let's begin with Barak. Some may give Barak a bad rap because he refused to go into battle without Deborah. It is possible that some of our common gender stereotypes unconsciously play into the perspective that he lacked valor. But was he actually a coward? I would argue that he respected her at a deep level and was smart and humble enough to want to collaborate with her. In fact, he needed her alongside. He knew his limitations and drew courage from going into battle alongside the strength and strategy of Deborah. Barak drew his courage from Deborah.

Then there is Lappidoth. Most of you had never heard of him until about five seconds ago. You are still attempting to pronounce his name. Give yourself grace. Your pronouncement of his name is not the critical part. However, understanding the meaning behind his name is important. Lappidoth is only mentioned briefly. He was Deborah's husband, and you might be tempted to just refer to him as "Mrs. Deborah." You would, however, be wrong.

His name gives us a clue about who he truly was. Lappidoth means "lighter of torches" or "fanner of flames." His name paints a picture of a spouse who fans into flames the gifts and destiny of his or her partner. That is no small thing, especially back then. In those patriarchal times, a husband had the right to forbid his wife from using her gifts. If he had, it would have blown up any chance for Deborah to lead her people. But Lappidoth was secure enough in who he was to allow his wife to soar.

Can I ask, do you have a Lappidoth? Do you have someone who breathes courage into you when you want to tap out of the "big thing" in front of you, when you want to take the easy route back down the steps instead of facing your Der Stuka moment? Is there a truth-teller or a champion in your life who, when you need that gentle (ok, that firm) kick towards God's purpose and plan, will gladly apply it to your backside?

If not, find one. If there is, free up their courage to speak boldly and purposefully into your life.

THE GUARDRAILS OF TYPE I COURAGE

In the midst of all the "fist-pumping, take the hill, let's start walking on water" mentality that comes naturally to *Type I's* like Peter, like Deborah, and perhaps like you, a word of caution. Courage, like any virtue, benefits from guidance and boundaries, much like guardrails on a road. These guardrails help steer our actions and decisions in a constructive direction, preventing recklessness or foolhardiness.

> IN ESSENCE, COURAGE WITH GUARDRAILS IS ABOUT THE TYPE I FINDING A BALANCE BETWEEN BOLDNESS AND WISDOM, BETWEEN TAKING RISKS AND EXERCISING CAUTION.

In essence, courage with guardrails is about the *Type I* finding a balance between boldness and wisdom, between taking risks and exercising caution. It's about navigating life's challenges with a clear sense of purpose, integrity, and consideration of yourself and others.

Having guardrails for courage means understanding the difference between bravery and impulsivity. It involves knowing when to act boldly and when to exercise caution. For instance, in a potentially dangerous situation that requires well-thought-out decisions and actions, courage with guardrails would assess the risks and take calculated steps rather than rushing in blindly.

When faced with a moral dilemma at work, courage with guardrails guides you to speak up against wrongdoing while prompting you to consider the most effective and ethical way to address the situation. You're mindful of potential consequences for yourself and others, and in this context, the guardrails of courage encourage you to take thoughtful action rather than acting impulsively.

Moreover, courage with guardrails requires a deep understanding of your values and principles. It means recognizing that bravery isn't just about taking risks but also about acting in alignment with your beliefs, even when it's challenging or uncomfortable. These guardrails help you stay true to yourself while navigating difficult circumstances.

Establishing guardrails for courage means embracing a willingness to learn and adapt. It means understanding that courage isn't a static trait, but a skill that can be continually developed over time. Courage is gained by always seeking feedback from others, reflecting and processing past experiences, and being open to new perspectives. By doing this, you can strengthen your courage while remaining grounded in humility and self-awareness. By embracing these guardrails, *Type I's* can navigate the complexities of life and leadership with confidence, purpose, and grace while having enough humility and self-awareness to fully recognize our limitations and blind spots.

COURAGE AS A HABIT

Here's why this is so relevant. Because 1300 years after Deborah's story and just a few years after Peter walked on water, another man who was being persecuted by Nero, would write to the Christians in Rome. Paul asked this group of Christians, *"If God is for us, who can be against us?" (Romans 8:31, NIV)*.

Today, the apostle Paul would say the same thing to all of us: God is with you and for you. So why wouldn't you wake up every day, filled with confidence from leaning on God, and courageously approach the moments and purposes God has put in front of you?

Do you want to know how you can wake up every day knowing God is for you? It's not by looking around from your seat in the boat at the personal waves rolling and threatening your comfortable life, or by watching the threat of things like finances, stress, resources, and relationship tension, bearing down into your world. And it's definitely not by looking around at culture. You've got to set your eyes on Jesus even as you take courageous steps daily.

What if you decided whatever role you had in life, you would approach it with the courage it requires? You could do that.

You're going to be a courageous...

... employee.

... boss.

... spouse.

... entrepreneur.

... giver of yourself.

... follower of Christ.

What if you just did this for a week? What if for just a week, every time you made a decision or were asked to do something, every time you had an opportunity to either merely sit it out or step up into a challenge, you asked the simple, but powerful question... *What would a courageous person do?* Especially a courageous person who had the confidence that God was beside them.

Type I's, let me boldly challenge you here. We can often substitute busyness for courage. We plow through life, make decisions randomly, and shake up every environment we walk into. Hidden beneath the blur activity can be a thread of fear. So let's align our tendency to plow through life vigorously with the God-given courage to operate intentionally and purposefully. How do we do that?

Every day, you should wake up, pause for just a moment, and ask, "What would a courageous person do with today, knowing that God is in, with, and for them?"

> **COURAGE IS NOT THE ABSENCE OF FEAR,
> IT IS CONFIDENCE IN THE PRESENCE OF GOD.**

Courage is not the absence of FEAR, it is confidence in the presence of GOD.

This simple daily question and reminder can channel your *Type I* wiring and ignite your higher calling.

This was the destiny Israel heard, the call Deborah answered, the moment Peter seized, and the life awaiting you. Embrace this habit, and I believe you'll embody the extraordinary *Type I* individual your heavenly Father envisioned.

He calls you to step out of the boat, to fix your gaze on Jesus, and to walk on water. Lean on Him, drawing courage that empowers you to fulfill your divine calling. That, my friend, is a thrilling and courageous way to live.

KEY TAKEAWAYS AND DISCUSSION STARTERS:

1. **COURAGE IN ACTION:** Courage is important when facing fears and stepping into the unknown. Though sometimes challenging to muster, courage is essential for *Type I* to embrace their extraordinary potential and respond boldly to life's opportunities.
- Can you talk about a time in your life when you responded boldly in the face of something that scared you?

2. **CHOOSING EXTRAORDINARY OVER ORDINARY:** There is a challenge we have as *Type I's* to resist settling for a mundane existence dictated by societal norms. Let's embrace the idea that we are courageous individuals with divine potential, and step out of comfort into the extraordinary adventure God has in store.
- Is there something extraordinary that you feel God calling you to? How can you take a step in that direction, knowing that it may be uncomfortable?

3. **COURAGE CONTRACTION:** Courage isn't about the absence of fear but about having confidence in God's presence.
- What practices or disciplines have you implemented into your life that can allow you to align with God's desire and plan? If you're not there yet, what are some areas of your life you need to invite God's presence into?

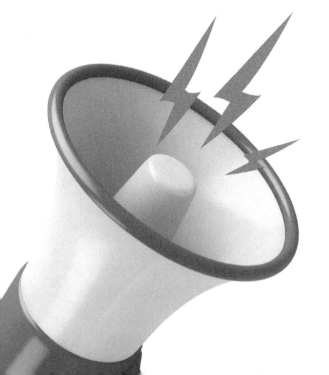

CHAPTER 6

CONTROL

Triggers.

Triggers cause a strong, negative emotional reaction. They can be things like fear, shock, anger, or worry. Usually, they happen suddenly, sparked by a seemingly unimportant or insignificant task. One of my key triggers is…waiting. While I'm self-aware enough to acknowledge this fact, it still triggers me when I'm forced to confront it.

Recently, I stole a key from the hotel my wife and I were staying at. It's fine. Go ahead. Judge me. I did it because I wanted a reminder of the amazing fiasco that it caused.

This past December, my wife and I stayed at one of our favorite hotels in New York City. If you're on staff at a church during the holidays, you know Christmas is a thing! So we make an annual getaway to our favorite city our "thing" before the Christmas crazy begins. It gives us a few days to have our own Christmas celebration, Plus, there's no better place than NYC at that time of year. The lights, snow, window displays…it's magical!

So we're staying in a nice, overpriced walk-in closet pretending to be a hotel room. This is not rare. It's how they do it in NYC. Ours happened to be on the twelfth floor near Midtown.

The hotel had a bank of four elevators with a digital control panel. To access the elevator, it was necessary to select exactly where you wanted to go, the lobby, restaurant, gym, or your room. Then the panel would tell you which corresponding elevator to use to go to that location. If the doors open and you just get on a random elevator, you won't necessarily end up where you want to go. In fact, there's no chance. It was a thing, but we got used to it.

However, on the last day of our trip, we packed up our bags and left them in our room. We went to a cute coffee shop nearby for one more cup of cortado and a pastry before we caught the train to the airport. Now, when you're on the twelfth floor, it takes a while for the elevator to arrive. So we are…waiting.

We finally caught the elevator, walked to the coffee shop, and enjoyed breakfast. As we were wrapping up, we realized we had to hurry to make the train to the airport. As we returned to the hotel, I reached in my pocket for the room key. Nothing. It was gone. I asked my wife if she had her key. She did! Great! Crisis averted.

We entered the lobby, went to the panel, selected our floor, and waited. The doors opened, we stepped inside and headed up to our floor. So far, so good. As we walked to our room, my wife took out the key that I was so grateful she had and we tapped the fancy door lock. Red light. We tapped again. The light was still red. I grabbed the key from her and tried it myself because, of course, my *Type I* can get this to work. I rapidly tapped the key. Red light. Red light. Red light. We were locked out.

We headed back to the elevators to go down to the lobby. We pushed the panel. We selected the lobby. We waited. (You're starting to see the trend here.) I calmly approached the front desk and with a very Christ-like tone said to the desk clerk, "Hey, our key isn't working and we need to get our bags and head to the airport." He apologized, made us a new key, and we made our way back upstairs.

As soon as we were back at our door, I started repeatedly tapping the lock again. You guessed it. Red light. Red light. Red light. My wife yanked the key from me. Red light. Red light. Red light. Same result. Now you would think this is the part of the story when, as we're standing on the 12th floor of a high-rise NYC hotel with our bags on one side of the door, a train departure time rapidly approaching and no access, we would start laughing and talk about what a great story this is going to make. Maybe the story might even make it into a book. I hate to disappoint you, but you would be terribly mistaken if that's what you thought. I was ready to blow a gasket.

We returned to the lobby where we explained to the same young man that the new key he'd just made still didn't work. We also made him *very* aware of the urgent need to get our bags so we wouldn't miss our train while trying my best to maintain my calm, which by this point was hanging on by a frayed thread. "Oh," he says apologetically. "The battery on your door lock must be dead. We'll send an engineer up to fix your door. You should go up and *wait* for the engineer to arrive." Long pause. Deep sigh.

We rode back up the elevator in silence. I'd done my best to keep my cool but inside I was hitting my max. As we sat in the hallway outside our door, my gut questioned if the guy at the front desk even called the engineer. On the other hand, my wife was waiting for the pressure-cooker *Type I* next to her to finally blow.

IF THERE'S ONE THING THAT UNITES TYPE I'S WITH EVERYONE ELSE IT'S THIS: WE ALL HAVE TO WAIT AND WE ALL HATE WAITING.

I was going to give it five minutes before taking more drastic measures, but to my surprise, the engineer appeared with a screwdriver in his hand. He quickly replaced the little batteries on the lock. Bingo. We were in! We grabbed our bags, thanked him, and ran to catch the train.

As I sat on the train heading to JFK, I chuckled about how triggered I was as I waited - as we tried our keys over and over, as we rode up and down the elevator, as we waited for the engineer to arrive - when in reality, we only waited a few minutes total and nothing catastrophic happened. We made our flight.

During the waiting, everything inside of me felt anxious and unsettled. Did anyone care? Was everyone oblivious to our situation? Why were they not moving faster? And what can I do to make all this better?

If there's one thing that unites *Type I's* with everyone else it's this: we all have to wait and we all hate waiting.

Waiting doesn't discriminate. It doesn't care if you're young or old, rich or poor, educated or uneducated. Everyone has to wait.

For *Type I's* the most painful thing about waiting is that it reminds us of one key fact: I am not in CONTROL.

You know it's true! You feel it whenever you have to wait for your spouse to finish getting ready so you can leave the house. Whenever you have to wait for the doctor to enter the exam room. Whenever you have to wait for traffic to move during rush hour. You're not in control. You are just... waiting.

A large amount of our lives is spent waiting. We try our best to avoid it. We honk at the car moving slower than we think it should. We switch lines at the store so we can check out faster. Confession. If you're like my family, we each get in a different line when entering a large venue. Whichever line moves fastest, is the line we all migrate towards. Don't judge. I know you do it too. Others are so eager to beat the church traffic in the parking lot or crowd at brunch that they skip the last song and "sneak" out of Sunday service early. You're not sneaky. We all see you.

If we're honest, we have to admit that our efforts to seek alternative pathways or try to avoid waiting altogether rarely work. Waiting is just a part of life. I mean think about it. How often have you moved from the "slow" line to the one moving faster just for the person in front of you to have an issue that results in your line coming to a screeching halt? You glance over to your original line and see the person who was behind you, finishing up and going on their merry way while you are stuck...waiting. For some of you, just reading this paragraph has stirred up some inner anxiety, annoyance, and frustration.

> DO YOU TRUST THAT WHAT GOD WANTS FOR YOUR LIFE
> IS BETTER THAN WHAT YOU WANT FOR YOUR LIFE?

Once we accept that waiting is inevitable, we can see that our perspective of control is actually a reflection of our relationship with God and how we trust Him. It makes you ask some tough questions like: Do you trust that what God wants for your life is better than what you want for your life?

THE ILLUSION OF CONTROL

The problem with waiting is that it's the antithesis of control, and *Type 1's* like to control. Actually, I'm going to edit that sentence. *Type 1's* like love to control. Or maybe: *Type 1's* ~~like love~~ need to control.

Whether you are a *Type 1* or not, you might have an issue with control. It's fairly rampant within the human experience. Not sure?

Let me share some red flags with you. You might be a control freak if…

- Your four favorite words are: "I told you so."
- Your three least favorite words: "I was wrong."
- Someone else driving = issue.
- Someone else holding the remote control = issue.
- You don't understand why no one else understands why you have your pantry color-coded.
- You don't have opinions. They're all facts.

> THE CHALLENGE WITH CONTROL IS THAT IT IS AN ILLUSION.

Maybe you're thinking, *Ohhh, I am a control freak.* If you're a *Type 1*, probably so. Part of our challenge as *Type 1's* is that we live and breathe the oxygen of control. We don't just want the optics of control, we deeply believe that if we are in control things will be better. For those of you who are led by or live with a *Type 1*, you secretly like us being in control. Yes, it drives you crazy at times. Yet, when the moment comes and someone needs to make a decision, react in a crisis, or lead the team, you're thrilled we are ready and willing to take over. Often you're left living in the tension between gratitude and frustration that naturally comes when living in proximity to a *Type I*.

The challenge with control is that it is an illusion. Control is temporary and micro in the world where God has placed us. We can control certain, smaller things for a bit, but ultimately control is outside our control. Interesting right?

We live in a culture that cultivates control issues. We're taught to be independent. That's a control issue. We're taught to do it yourself. That's a control issue. We want to be in charge. Yep, another control issue. We believe we can have all the information and answers we need. The reality is our world is unpredictable. We live believing that we have more control because we have more information. We don't.

However, we can't stand the thought that we might not be in control. We crave control. So much so that we imagine we have control even when we don't. Psychologist Ellen Langer calls this the "illusion of control."[1] The illusion provides a false sense of security until something happens and it shatters.

- A driver misses a stop sign.
- A spouse says, "I don't love you anymore."
- A doctor gives a diagnosis that leaves you in disbelief.
- A child rebels.
- A boss says, "We're having to lay off some people. I'm sorry."

Instantly, your true level of control (or lack thereof) becomes crystal clear. As a coping mechanism, we find creative ways to hold on to some sense of control. Jennifer Dukes, in her book, *It's All Under Control*, interprets our craving for control as us believing, "I'm safer and more secure if I'm in charge."[2]

But there's a dark side to craving this level of control. For me, it looks like this.

It's 2:30 am. I'm traveling. Consistent travel means you become somewhat used to random, routine hotel rooms which is exactly where I found myself a few months ago. The room was cold, very cold. Why? Because I'm that guy who immediately cranks the AC to 65°F when walking into a hotel room because I paid for cold air and that's how I love to sleep. That night, I was shaking under the blankets, not from the cold, but from the anxiety of being completely overwhelmed. My heart raced with that wide-awake, mind-spinning feeling. Everyone has these moments, but I believe *Type I's* are a bit more susceptible.

On this particular night, it wasn't one thing that woke me up, started the spinning, and left me shaking as I stared past the mass-produced bland hotel art on the wall and out the window. It wasn't even multiple things. It was the fact that all the items going through my brain were uncontrollable. A friend had recently lost his young wife after a long battle with cancer. A staff member had suddenly decided to leave our team for a new opportunity. My son was wrestling with some new direction in his life. Another friend's marriage was starting to fray. I couldn't solve, fix, or control any of it. The real challenge wasn't each of those very challenging circumstances. It was my inability to navigate it.

Crisis doesn't phase me. Lack of control *spins* me.

Bad. Perhaps you can relate.

THE COST OF CONTROL

Although we would hate to admit it, there are consequences to our insatiable need for control. Things like:

Anxiety

As a *Type I*, we have to know everything, do everything, and be in charge of everything. That's a lot! Yet, we'd rather carry the weight of responsibility than risk uncertainty. We'd rather live with the illusion of control because when our illusion of control is shattered it creates a level of anxiety that we don't know how to manage.

The irony is that we think we're anxious because we don't have enough control when, in fact, we're trying to control too much. It's like we're trying to treat the sickness with its cause.

Exhaustion

Being in control is exhausting, feeling like you always have to be in the driver's seat. It's a lot of pressure. You have to ensure everything is moving forward, that everything works out right, that every problem is solved quickly, and that everyone is okay.

> **LIVING AS THOUGH ALL OF LIFE DEPENDS ON YOU AND YOUR STRENGTH IS AN ILLUSION, AND IT'S NOT GOD'S PLAN FOR US.**

Living as though all of this depends on you and your strength is an illusion, and it's not God's plan for us. We are not wired to carry it all. To some, it may seem as though *Type I's* thrive under that level of intensity. The truth is over time, it wears on us and can lead to burnout.

Fraud

We not only attempt to exert control over every aspect and individual in our lives, but we also strive to manipulate the optics others have about us. Seeking approval and admiration, we carefully curate our public image, which also ramps up our anxiety. Deep down, we are aware of our inability to govern every circumstance. Yet, we hide this vulnerability, working extremely hard to uphold a facade of control through our competence and composure. This relentless effort drains us and undermines our effectiveness as leaders and followers of Christ.

Resentment

Where control really gets...well, out of control... is when our desire to influence how others perceive us crosses the line into attempting to control their thoughts and emotions, that's when things truly spiral out of control. People inherently resist being manipulated or dominated; it breeds resentment over time. Even if you believe you're acting as a savior, heroically attempting to steer others' lives, the reality is actually different. Spoiler alert: it never ends well.

This tendency might even be at the root of challenges in your relationships, perhaps with your spouse, kids, or employees. If you find yourself regularly identifying with this dangerous controlling *Type I* shadow side, you're likely nodding in agreement right now or at least quietly acknowledging its truth. Regardless of intentions, controlling behavior eventually suffocates those around you.

God Complex

Our relationship with God reflects the biggest cost to a control addiction. God is all-knowing, all-powerful, never-changing. He is always in control. He can always be trusted. According to Deuteronomy, *"He is the Rock, his works are perfect, and all his ways are just. A faithful God who does no wrong, upright and just is he." (Deuteronomy 32:4, NIV)*

It is so encouraging to me to read that description of God. He is perfect, He's a rock, He doesn't change, He doesn't move, and He's a firm foundation. He's just. He does no wrong. He's upright. That is the kind of God we follow. He is FAITHFUL. He can be trusted if we release our false assumption that we are in control and desire to control everything.

IF GOD IS ALL-KNOWING, ALL-POWERFUL, SHOULDN'T I WANT TO SERVE HIM MORE THAN I WANT HIM TO SERVE ME?

As followers of Jesus, we're supposed to place our trust in God. Instead, we often put our faith more in ourselves, somehow falling for the lie that things will be better if we are in control.

When we fall into this trap of gripping tightly to every aspect of our lives, we miss out on what a real relationship with God is like, what it could be, and what it could do in our lives. As a result, we settle for average when God wants to give us abundant.

He wants to lead us. He has plans for our lives. If we stay in control, He can't be in control. It's one or the other. Consequently, we miss out on His bigger, better plans.

In case you think I'm pointing fingers, I'll confess. I do this most often in my prayer life. A quick analysis of my frequent prayers would conclude that most of them consist of me telling God what I need, when I need it, and the best way for Him to do it. Yes, God invites me to ask Him for things. He's cool with that. But, if He's all-knowing, all-powerful, shouldn't I want to serve Him more than I want Him to serve me? Shouldn't I be more interested in asking questions than giving directions?

This is what it means to be a Christian, to trust that the God who created the stars in the sky, the beauty we see around us, and breathed air into our lungs is the same God who wants to lead us where He's going. The problem is we want God, but we also want to be in control. We want to be the writer, director, and star of our story. But Jesus says, *"If you cling to your life, you will lose it; but if you give up your life for me, you will find it"* (Matthew 10:39, NIV).

NOT MY MENTALITY

Jesus didn't just speak about this. He lived it. He, too, had a moment when He wrestled with allowing His Heavenly Father to be in total control. It was the moment that changed the course of eternity. You might assume it would be easy for Jesus, being God in the flesh, to trust His Father and surrender control. It wasn't. In His humanity, Jesus, facing His darkest moment, felt control slipping away.

It happened the night before Jesus was crucified.

Jesus invited Peter and two other disciples to go with Him to the Garden of Gethsemane, one of His favorite places to pray. Peter, who as a *Type I*, had already experienced a string of control issues resulting in some uncomfortable situations. We've documented a few of these already, but for the sake of review, let's go there one more time.

There was the conversation when Jesus announced to His disciples that He was destined to die, and Peter boldly corrected Him. *No Jesus, I won't let that happen.* Why? Because Peter just knew he could keep things under control. Then, there was the awkward moment when Peter tried to take over the supernatural situation on the mount of transfiguration. *Yes, I realize I'm here with Moses, Elijah, and the Son of God, but I kinda think I should be in charge, and my idea is to build everyone little houses to sleep in.*

Again, Peter is gripping tightly to what he assumes is God's plan while missing the point altogether. That's what an unhealthy relationship with control will do. While we stubbornly hold on to our desired direction or solution, God is moving in an entirely different way, and we risk missing it. *Type I's* are powerful leaders whom God has wired to take charge. But our take charge instinct must be tempered with our ultimate deference to God's plans and desires.

As the night settles in, the group arrives at the garden, fatigued from the day's events. Despite the weariness, Jesus pleads with His three disciples to lift Him up in prayer while He retreats to pray alone. Why did Jesus seek solitude? *"My soul is overwhelmed with sorrow to the point of death,"* he reveals. *"Stay here and keep watch with me"* (Matthew 26:38, NIV). Jesus' soul is so crushed with grief and engulfed by sorrow that His only recourse is to get alone.

While some believe that Jesus' suffering began on the cross or during the physical torture preceding crucifixion, the truth is that it originated right here, in the Garden of Gethsemane. He felt an overwhelming sense of the journey ahead—its physical toll and the enormous self-sacrifice it would demand. Let's not overlook the reality that relinquishing control always necessitates significant self-sacrifice. It's a real struggle for us, just as it was for Jesus.

RELINQUISHING CONTROL ALWAYS
NECESSITATES SIGNIFICANT SELF-SACRIFICE.

We catch a glimpse of this reality from the depth and content of Jesus' prayer as He slipped away alone to a quiet place in the garden. Matthew tells us, *"Going a little farther, He fell with His face to the ground and prayed, 'My Father, if it is possible, may this cup be taken from me. Yet not as I will, but as you will.'"* (Matthew 26:39, NIV).

Jesus is fully aware of what will happen the next day. He knows He will be tortured, mocked, humiliated, rejected, and then crucified. Many consider crucifixion to be the most excruciating way for a person to die. In fact, we get the word "excruciating" from the word crucifixion.

But that's not the main thing Jesus is dreading. Even worse than what Jesus will experience physically is what He will go through spiritually. He held the weight of the world's sins as He hung on the cross. Jesus, who had never sinned or experienced a moment of separation from His Father, took on all of our sins, and in doing so became separated from His Father for the first time.

That was the worst part.

The idea of it crushes Jesus. He pleads, "Father, is there any other way?"

Did you catch the significance of two words in Jesus' prayer? "If" and "yet." Jesus prays, "If it is possible … yet not as I will." Throughout the night, Jesus will grapple with the tension between "if" and "yet."

This reveals that praying for God to intervene in our circumstances is acceptable. "God, if it's possible for this situation to change, please change it." However, true surrender occurs in the "yet." "Yet, not my will, but yours be done, God." It happens when we can say, "God, this is my request, but I will always submit to what you know is best for me."

The reality is that you can't control every outcome or situation, but you can choose to surrender. God can accomplish far more through your surrender than you could ever achieve through control.

> GOD CAN ACCOMPLISH FAR MORE THROUGH YOUR SURRENDER
> THAN YOU COULD EVER ACHIEVE THROUGH CONTROL.

WHEN SURRENDER IS EVERYTHING

That's precisely where Jesus found himself in the Garden of Gethsemane.

The fate of our salvation hung precariously in the balance between the "if" and the "yet." Aren't you thankful Jesus didn't yield to His own desires at that moment? Aren't you relieved He desperately grappled with the tension between the "if" and the "yet," ultimately choosing the "yet"? He chose God's will. He chose us. He chose you.

Jesus teaches us a crucial principle in the garden: what transpires between the "if" and the "yet" in our lives is critical. It's in that moment of decision, prayer, and action that our relationship with control is fully exposed. *Type I's* need to deeply embed this in our hearts as we wrestle with control.

So, let's revisit the question: Would you rather pursue your will for your life or God's will? While we may naturally desire our own preferences, our ultimate desire should be aligned with God's. If we lack this attitude and neglect to pray this prayer, we may label ourselves as followers of Jesus, but in honesty, we might not truly be following Him.

Choosing to follow Jesus marks just the beginning of our journey. For those wired as *Type I*, this should serve as an inspiration. It's the point where God begins His transformative work within us. *Type I* individuals often struggle between confidence in their innate wiring and a willingness to yield to God's transforming power. And when we surrender control, be prepared—God will do precisely that: transform us.

God will grow some things in you, reorder, rewire, and remove some things. He wants His character to start showing up in your life over and over and over again. And I'm telling you, it is an absolute game changer when God starts growing His character in us.

Now, I also want you to know that there is actually not a version of following Jesus that doesn't include radical character change. It's part of it. You're going to notice a change. People around you are going to notice. They're going to say, "You're different. Something has changed." Or at least they should.

Let me gently say here that if you consider yourself a follower of Jesus, but you cannot point to any character change and no one in your life can point to any difference in the way that you act or the way you treat people, I have to say, in love of course, that it may not be Jesus that you are following. It may be yourself. It may be someone else. Because following Jesus ALWAYS includes radical character change. Even if you've followed Him since childhood -even for us *Type I's*... ESPECIALLY for *Type I's* - there should be ongoing transformation.

If that character change is lacking, it's possible we are not living within a full, growing relationship with Jesus. Instead, we're probably living out something called: moralistic therapeutic deism. What's that? It's a description that few, if any, Christians probably know, but it truly describes what many are doing. Here's the basics of the term:

- Moralistic: to be a good person.
- Therapeutic: to feel better about yourself.
- Deism: a belief that God exists, but is not regularly involved in your life.

A lot of people believe that Christianity is merely about being a nice person so that a mostly uninvolved God will make your life better with an end goal of happiness. That is *not* the gospel. That's *not* Christianity. In fact, it's the *opposite*.

Many mistakenly equate Christianity with simply being nice to attract blessings from a distant God, aiming for personal happiness. However, this notion starkly contrasts the essence of the gospel. True Christianity involves recognizing our sinful nature and our profound need for a Savior. It necessitates complete surrender, releasing control, to Jesus' lordship and guidance, with the ultimate objective being His will, not ours.

When we pray for *our* will to be done, we practice moralistic therapeutic deism. We're following *ourselves* into the lives we have for us.

When we pray, "Not my will, but yours be done," we're following Jesus' example into the life *God* has for us.

And the life God has for us is *better* and *bigger*. Trust me.

BETTER AND BIGGER

Although relinquishing control is undeniably difficult, there are two compelling reasons why we should allow God to lead.

First of all, God's will for your life is *better* than your will for your life.

Do you know that God loves you more than you love you? It's true. That's why he wants to lead you into *"His good, pleasing, and perfect will." (Romans 12:2, NIV)*. Sometimes, His plan may diverge significantly from what we had envisioned. In fact, more often than not, this is the case. Accepting His goodness can be particularly challenging when His answer is "no." Jesus, Himself, struggled to accept His Father's "no" when He pleaded for an alternative way to redeem the world.

DO YOU KNOW THAT GOD LOVES YOU MORE THAN YOU LOVE YOU?

Yet, like Jesus, we must learn to trust that God's timing and methods are always superior to our own. When God's response is "no," we must trust Him because He sees the entire completed picture while we see only a fleeting snapshot. God is inherently good, His promises are true, and He is entirely trustworthy.

Secondly, God's will for your life is *bigger* than your will for your life.

Why did God deny Jesus? Because He had a grander purpose in mind than Jesus' immediate comfort. Jesus' ultimate mission, God's overarching plan for Him, was to provide a pathway to salvation and reconcile us with our Heavenly Father.

The same principle applies to each of us. God has unique and precise plans for our lives. As *Type I* individuals, it can be challenging to comprehend that His pace and process could lead to a bigger plan than what we've envisioned for ourselves, our teams, and the organizations we lead. Yet, that's precisely what God accomplishes.

I'm reminded of the words in *Jeremiah 29:11, NIV: "'For I know the plans I have for you,' declares the Lord."* So often, we quote this familiar verse without fully grasping the depths of its truth. God's plans for us are not just good. They are bigger, better, expansive, and superior to our own.

You and I should be glad for that.

God's overarching plan injects our lives with purpose and excitement, but (and here's the significant "but") it can also be terrifying —much like a roller coaster ride.

Personally, I detest roller coasters. No, you don't understand. I HATE roller coasters. Is it because they're fast? Nope. Is it because of the towering heights and stomach-churning drops? No. It's not about the speed or the death-defying plunges. It's about the loss of control. Want to cure my fear of roller coasters immediately? Put a steering wheel in my seat. Let me drive. I might even guide us along the same path we would have taken anyway, but at least it would be my choice. I'd know our destination and the pace I prefer.

Sure, God's plan is bigger and better, but it can also feel frightening because you don't know exactly where God will lead you and you're not privy to His timing. You have to give up control. You have to set aside your agenda and your will. *Type I's* are squirming right now just processing the idea of releasing our tight grip on our lives.

It's risky because you don't know what God's will for you might be. You have some ideas. You have your calling, but the rest is still TBD. That's where we get a good idea of where our faith truly lies.

IN THE FACE OF UNCERTAINTY

The author of Hebrews reminds us that *"Faith is the substance of things hoped for, the evidence of things unseen" (Hebrews 11:1, NIV).* I think faith also means wanting what God wants for you more than what you may want for yourself and walking in obedience to God into an unknown future. A faithful life is a life of trusting God in the face of uncertainty.

> A FAITHFUL LIFE IS A LIFE OF TRUSTING GOD
> IN THE FACE OF UNCERTAINTY.

We have to give up control, which is terrifying for control addicts. The great Christian thinker and author Henri Nouwen wrote, *"One of the most arduous spiritual tasks is that of giving up control and allowing the Spirit of God to lead our lives."*[3]

The irony lies in the fact that we never truly possessed control to begin with. Remember, control is merely an illusion. Despite our desires and assumptions, we can't predict with absolute certainty what the future holds. We may crave that certainty and believe we have it, but ultimately, it is a mystery.

Who knows what will happen a year from now? Let's be honest. You don't even know what will happen tomorrow! You have your plans, meetings, hopes, and objectives, but all our planning cannot control what actually happens. It is a glorious and frustrating mystery.

James writes about this kind of false confidence; the imagery is fitting and powerful. Eugene Peterson's paraphrase captures it so thoroughly, *"And now I have a word for you who brashly announce, "Today—at the latest, tomorrow— (I have to* think James has some *Type I's* in mind as he writes this) *we're off to such and such a city for the year. We're going to start a business and make a lot of money."* You don't know the first thing about tomorrow. You're nothing but a wisp of fog, catching a brief bit of sun before disappearing. Instead, make it a habit to say, "If the Master wills it and we're still alive, we'll do this or that." (James 4:14, MSG).

Our lives, while valuable, are brief and completely dependent on God's grace. Like your breath on a frigid winter day, our lives reveal themselves briefly only to vanish quickly. This reality shouldn't leave us depressed, but rather motivated. We've been given this one singular life, designed by God for a very specific purpose, and any illusion of control we have is simply ridiculous. So if we never really had control in the first place, are we actually giving it up? I don't think so. Instead, we're relinquishing the illusion of control, the false sense of mastery over our circumstances.

In the classic work *The Screwtape Letters*, C.S. Lewis vividly depicts a senior demon instructing younger demons on the art of tempting humans and keeping them from the lives God intends for them. Who knew that demons had masterclasses?

In one particular lesson, the senior demon explains that humans seldom utter the one prayer God truly desires to hear: "Not my will, but yours be done." Instead, they will pray that God will help them through their struggles. The senior demon goes on to say that people don't experience real life with God because they persist in wrapping their anxious hands around life's steering wheel, convinced that if they hold on tighter, everything will somehow fall into place.

I love to hold a tight grip on things. Many of you do as well. For a number of years, my daughter Ashlee was deeply involved in competitive softball and found her way to the pitching mound. Pitching means she was at the center of it all when her team was in the field. I secretly (and sometimes loudly) enjoyed her being at the center of the action) As a *Type I*, it also meant I was deeply and sometimes sadistically wanting to control the results. Who doesn't as a parent? Your daughter is standing in front of everyone, gripping and unwrapping the ball, staring at a catcher's mitt 45 feet away, and listening to the coach and the crowd screaming at her.

Looking back, she was so courageous, and I was so controlling—at least in any way I could. Because I was not the one throwing the ball, I could merely scream encouragement over and over again. She took it (probably knew I was a *Type I* though she didn't have a label for it), but there were moments when she made eye contact with me and without words said, "Dad. Enough."

Listen, parental control is a real phenomenon and *Type I* parental control is often next level. My daughter survived, but in hindsight, I appreciate her willingness to put up with her crazy, overly-zealous father. (I may need to call her and apologize again.)

Frankly, giving up control is scary. It's daunting and unsettling. So let's reframe how we think and feel about letting go of control. Instead of seeing control as something we're relinquishing, let's embrace the unknown and lack of control as a thrilling challenge that leads to adventure.

If you're willing to let Jesus lead, He will guide you to places you never could've imagined and down paths you never knew existed.

Is that unnerving? Sure. But … it's also exhilarating. Your life is now out of your hands. Someone else is leading you.

And not just anyone. This someone loves you while having a better and bigger plan for your life. You don't know what will happen, but you know it won't be boring.

If you find your life or relationship with God boring, consider the possibility that you've settled for something less than what God intends for you. Perhaps you've inadvertently invited Him to follow your lead rather than the other way around. Instead of allowing the Spirit to guide you, you're charting your own course, hoping the Spirit will tag along. As a result, you experience spiritual stagnation and boredom rather than spiritual adventure.

Instead, release it and give yourself permission to embrace the crazy, marvelous, and unknown adventure of "hands-free" living.

KEY TAKEAWAYS AND DISCUSSION STARTERS:

· · · · · · · · · · ·

1. THE ILLUSION OF CONTROL: Humans tend to crave control. Control is an illusion that leads to anxiety, exhaustion, and a sense of being an imposter.

- Describe a recent time when you realized your lack of control over life's events.
- What would it look like for you to pursue a life of surrender?

2. SURRENDERING TO GOD'S CONTROL: Jesus' experience in the Garden of Gethsemane serves as a powerful lesson on the importance of surrendering control to God's will. Despite facing overwhelming circumstances, Jesus grappled with the idea of relinquishing control but ultimately chose to submit to God's plan, even at great personal sacrifice.

- Talk about a time in your life when you let go of a situation and you watched as God worked it out.
- What does it look like to align your desires with God's greater plan and purpose?

3. GOD'S WILL: God's will surpasses our own in both quality and scope. His plan, though often different from what we envision, leads to more fulfilling and purposeful outcomes. Embracing God's will requires stepping into the unknown with faith, and trusting in His overarching plan for our lives.

- Can you pinpoint a time in your life that required stepping into the unknown?
- Describe how you feel you may have grown from an uncomfortable moment in your life.

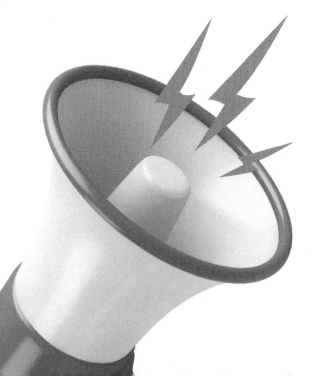

CHAPTER 7

CONCEITED

．．．．．．．．．．．．

Whether you consider yourself a *Type I* or not, most of us share two common traits of the human experience: we all try hard to appear that we have it all together, and we often carry ourselves with an inappropriate swagger. I know this because I do it. I do it often. I do it way too often.

This is especially true if you find yourself in a position of authority or influence, or simply standing on a stage with an audience who chooses to listen to you. All of this can mess with and confuse the average person. For a *Type I,* the temptation to elevate yourself is typically stronger. Conceit becomes a byproduct of the illusion of control, which we've covered extensively. Conceit manifests itself with the idea that I am more important than anyone else.

If you don't believe me, take a moment to reflect on your driving experience. Put someone behind the wheel of a vehicle and immediately their level of pride or lack thereof will emerge. Do you feel like you own the road or do you yield to others? Don't believe me?

Ponder the last time you were on the freeway. The road is packed. Traffic is slow. Orange cones are everywhere because construction is happening. As you analyze the situation, your frustration level rises. (Note: I am using 'your' because I'm growing weary of making personal confessions. However, if it makes you feel better, feel free to substitute "Lee" for "your".)

You realize that traffic is merging. However, there is an opportunity to delay your merge and continue up the open lane.

Never mind that in just a short distance, you will be forced to merge anyway. Never mind that everyone else is patiently waiting and staying in the open lane. Never mind that it is a "me first, I am in a hurry, it is my world, and you're just living in" move to speed down the lane and then wedge yourself into the lane.

I recall making this move once when our daughter Ashlee was learning to drive. She was shocked, baffled, and disgusted as I sped around the lane to force my way into the flow. She is way more honorable and humble than I am. It was a "do as I say, not as I do" moment for sure. While I did manage to wedge myself three cars ahead of my original spot, it was definitely not my proudest parenting moment.

Of course, in the midst of that move, I wasn't thinking, "I might have a pride issue." My only concern was getting to my destination quickly. But at its core, moves like this are rooted in pride. This is a pretty benign example of how it plays out, but perhaps it is the seemingly benign moments of conceit that build and blind us.

IT IS THE SEEMINGLY BENIGN MOMENTS
OF CONCEIT THAT BUILD AND BLIND US.

In her bestseller, *The Year of Magical Thinking*, Joan Didion attempted to make sense of her husband's sudden death. The couple had just returned home from visiting their daughter in the hospital where their only child was in a coma (she would die a year later). They sat down for dinner when Joan's husband died of a massive coronary.

The book's title refers to her awareness that she kept behaving as though her husband would come back - if she didn't give away his clothes and if she could find out as much info as possible regarding his death - then it didn't really happen. He wasn't gone. She knew better, but could not keep these irrational thoughts from controlling her.

She describes how people (like her, perhaps like you, and definitely like *Type I's*) operate when she relates,

> *"They believe absolutely in their own management skills. They believed absolutely in the power of the telephone numbers they had at their fingertips; the right doctor, the major donor, the person who could facilitate a favor. I had myself for most of my life shared the same core belief in my ability to control events. Yet... some events just happen. This was one of those events. You sit down to dinner and life as you know it ends."[1]*

In the end, she concludes, we are all powerless. She's not wrong, but for those of us who are pursuing Jesus, being powerless means our obsession with ourselves must give way to an obsession with a posture that clearly concludes GOD IS GOD... AND WE ARE NOT.

GOD IS GOD... AND WE ARE NOT.

I know we all have to pause right now and wrestle with that. The *Type I's* should pause even longer. I get it. In theory and theology, we know that, but in practice, it is often lost on us.

Notice that the following truth appears three times in scripture. If you are wondering whether that is normal, it is not. In fact, it is the only time this happens. Also, notice that Peter reminds us that *"God opposes the proud, but shows favor to the humble"* (James 4:6, 1 Peter 5:5, Proverbs 3:34, NIV).

FACT #1: IF YOU ARE PROUD, GOD IS OPPOSING YOU.

It's not that He doesn't love you. In fact, He loves you more than you can imagine. However, it's very difficult to break through your conceit so that He can fully use you.

FACT #2: IF YOU HUMBLE YOURSELF, GOD WILL FAVOR YOU.

Does that mean you are his favorite? It does not. Favor means the presence of humility will open the door for God to fully leverage your skills, talents, and God-given abilities. In a sense, Jesus wants to give you life to its fullest, but our pride and self-absorption can get in the way.

Solomon (also a big *Type I*) struggled quite a bit with pride. He often placed himself at the center of the universe. He observed correctly that *"Pride goes before destruction, a haughty spirit before a fall." (Proverbs 16:18, NIV)*. The Message paraphrase of this verse goes further and doesn't pull any punches. *"First Pride, then the crash - the bigger the ego, the harder the fall" (Proverbs 16:18, The MSG).* This imagery vividly underscores the seriousness with which God views the presence of unhealthy pride.

I've experienced a couple of vehicle accidents. Each time, it feels as if everything slows down just before impact. You're cruising along, then suddenly there's an object or another car, and it's like slow motion before BAM—the crash. Pride operates in the same way; it blinds you, and before you realize it, pride sets off a chain reaction that can ultimately devastate your life.

We can recall numerous individuals who appeared to be incredibly successful, only to experience a crash-and-burn downfall because they seemed to believe they were invulnerable: Michael Milken, Martha Stewart, Anthony Weiner, Jack Abramoff, Harvey Weinstein, Elizabeth Holmes, Jeffrey Epstein, David Petraeus, Kevin Spacey, Ken Lay, Deshaun Watson, Bernie Madoff, and—in my local community—Steve Wynn, and—in my pastoral profession—well, that list is unfortunately way too long. The point is clear: God wasn't joking when He warned that pride precedes a fall. We witness it all around us.

The "crash" mentioned in Proverbs doesn't occur suddenly and unexpectedly. On the journey toward destruction, there's typically a gradual, depressing decline. Arthur C. Brooks writes about this in his book *From Strength to Strength*. He describes years of studying the lives and biographies of highly motivated, highly successful people. He then writes:

What I found was a hidden source of anguish that wasn't just widespread but nearly universal among people who have done well in their careers. I came to call this the "strivers curse": people who strive to be excellent at what they do often wind up finding their inevitable decline terrifying, their successes increasingly unsatisfying, and their relationships lacking."

"And if you ... have worked hard to be exceptional at what you do, you will almost certainly face a similar pattern of decline and disappointment – and it will come much, much sooner than you think."[2]

SIGNATURE SIN

The warnings about pride are crucial for everyone to hear and take to heart, but they carry particular significance for us *Type I's*, as pride tends to be our signature sin. We traffic in pride like a cupcake shop owner traffics in flour and icing. Pride comes naturally to us. It's our specialty. While we might often wear it as a badge of honor, it shouldn't be. When pride is our signature sin, we need to be acutely aware of its presence.

When considering the pattern of infamous, prideful lives being destroyed, you might wonder how many of them were *Type I's*. I couldn't say for sure, but my guess would be around 99%, and even that might be conservative. To clarify, I firmly believe that pride is a universal human issue, but *Type I* individuals seem to be predisposed to have a greater struggle.

At its core, pride is a double-edged sword of healthy and unhealthy character. Healthy pride encompasses self-confidence and purposeful motivation, acknowledging our individual gifts while recognizing them as God-given. On the other hand, conceit represents the unhealthy version of self-worth that, when left unchecked, can be incredibly destructive. Excessive pride leads to narcissism and arrogance, promoting a cycle of self-destructive behavior.

In Philippians 2, the Apostle Paul writes to a church full of Christians encouraging them to *"Do nothing out of selfish ambition or vain conceit" (Philippians 2:3, NIV).*

Selfish ambition means it's about me. It carries an idea of competitiveness. Not only is everything about me, but I desperately want to be better than you. Paul instructs us not to live this way. He says there is to be <u>no</u> selfish ambition or vain conceit. In fact, he says if you did something "in vain" you did it for nothing. It's worthless. Paul wants us to understand it's not all about you.

It's *so* easy to live like the world is a movie, and I'm the star with everyone else making guest appearances. We inadvertently do it all the time. Here's a really silly, but eye-opening example of this:

When someone takes a group photo you're in, who do you look for first when you see the picture? Yourself. And if you look bad, you think, "It's a bad picture." If you look good, it's a good picture. In fact, it's a great picture. Actually, you're going to post that all over your social media even if everyone else looks terrible. One person can have their eyes closed, another is caught mid-sneeze while the third has a nasty piece of spinach in their teeth, but if you look good, that's all that matters. You're posting that awesome picture. That's a little vain conceit working overtime.

Type I's major in selfish ambition and vain conceit, but Paul warns against it and offers the healthy alternative, *"Rather, in humility value others above yourselves" (Philippians 2:3, NIV).*

Paul goes on to say, *"not looking to your own interests but each of you to the interests of the others." (Philippians 2:4, NIV).* Who would choose to live this way?

Jesus.

It may seem counterintuitive, but this is the way Jesus lived. And as His followers, Paul encourages us to *"have the same mindset as Christ Jesus" (Philippians 2:5, NIV).*

BEING A CHRISTIAN IS NOT MERELY BELIEVING
IN JESUS. IT'S FOLLOWING HIS EXAMPLE.

Being a Christian is not merely believing in Jesus. It's following His example. When you and I choose to follow Him, we choose to lead the life He led…and Jesus didn't live for himself. He humbled himself and lived for others.

So why is pride often such a struggle for us *Type I* individuals?

> **I BELIEVE ONE OF THE DRIVING FORCES FOR A TYPE I IS A STRONG NEED TO BE SPECIAL.**

I believe one of the driving forces for a *Type I* is a strong need to be special. There's something in us that looks at those comfortably cruising through life, showing up at the same place every day and doing it with complete contentment as amazing. But, it's also a little strange to us. We observe and even admire it, but can't fathom how someone would not feel the need to strive, to grasp, to reach for something more.

We tell ourselves we're not judging them. It's just that we don't understand them. If we're brutally honest with ourselves, we do judge them. Our pride causes us to view them as less than—less motivated, less ambitious, less important, and even less successful. We then put ourselves on a shaky pedestal. Friend, that pedestal is a dangerous place to stand.

One of the driving factors for a *Type I's* condescending attitude towards those who seem less motivated is a strong desire to feel special. Often this drive supersedes all others. Left unchecked, it becomes intoxicating and dangerous.

Arthur Brooks writes of an encounter he had with a successful financier. She was frustrated with the state of her life so Brooks finally asked her why she didn't just fix the sources of her unhappiness by taking time to work on her marriage, spend time with her family, and rest and recuperate physically. It seems logical that if you are miserable you would want to fix the source of the misery if you could isolate it.

Brooks relates what happened next. *"She thought about my question for a couple of minutes. Finally, she looked at me and said, matter-of-factly, "Maybe I would prefer to be **special** rather than happy." Looking at my astonished face, she explained: "Anyone can do the things it takes to be happy—go on vacation, spend time with friends and family . . . but not everyone can accomplish great things."*[3]

Her issue came from the fact that her hand-crafted ideal version of herself was incomplete. Essentially, she had exchanged her true self for a mere symbol of herself to remain special. As a result, she was unhappily special.

GODLY AMBITION

In her book, *Strengthening the Soul of Your Leadership*, Ruth Haley Barton says,

"Some people seem to make it through life without ever having to wrestle with the fatal question. They seem to move through life with ease - making a living, enjoying the fruits of their labor, taking what seems to be an easy or at least a rather clearly marked path to security and success - while others seem to be called to make commitments that require us to do strange things and orient our lives toward realities that others do not even see. It is hard to be this kind of person - to have a fire burning within us that we can't 'shut up in our bones' without doing damage to the soul. It's hard to keep answering a calling that continually takes us right to the edge of our faith and our human limitations. Sometimes we are tempted to feel resentful."[4]

The passage resonated with me so profoundly that I captured a screenshot of the page, which now resides in my favorites folder on my phone. While others may have breezed past this paragraph, her words stunned me and caused me to pause. I deeply identified with the exhilarating yet sometimes frustrating sensation that I can't simply coast through life; nearly every day feels like an opportunity to make significant contributions to the world. I wake up each day with the conviction that I'm ultimately on a significant assignment. It charges me up while also making vain conceit a lurking threat. There is a fine line between partnering with God's plan for the world in small ways and pushing our agenda on the world in big ways.

THERE IS A FINE LINE BETWEEN PARTNERING WITH GOD'S PLAN FOR THE WORLD IN SMALL WAYS AND PUSHING OUR AGENDA ON THE WORLD IN BIG WAYS.

It's a universal desire to feel valued, to belong, and to believe one is unique. However, this longing runs much deeper for *Type I's*—it's like a burning passion within us.

If you're anything like me, you might find yourself slightly offended when reading the Bible's advice to: *"make it your ambition to lead a quiet life: You should mind your own business and work with your hands" (1 Thessalonians 4:11, NIV).* A quiet life! That sounds suffocating. After all, who aspires to lead a quiet life? A *Type I* yearns for a life filled with excitement and dynamism—a loud, rocket ship kind of life.

So, what exactly is Godly ambition? Is it even possible? Lance Witt, pastor and author, felt that existing definitions fell short, so he devised his own. Developing your own definition is a characteristic *Type I* move, but in this case, it's powerful.

Witt defines ambition as, "a sustained, preoccupying, driving, intense desire to achieve something.[5] Sustained means it isn't fleeting. Preoccupied refers to the fact you are obsessed and your mind can't stop thinking about it. Driving refers to the hard push ambition gives toward action. And finally, intense desire refers to living with passion in an inherently God-driven direction.

To some extent, each of us should possess the healthy ambition God instilled in us. Ambition isn't exclusive to *Type I's*. It's that force that drives us, the burning in the belly that ignites us, and the catalyst that can even prompt us to make significant sacrifices, particularly when they align with God's mission in the world. When our ambition originates from God and we actively seek His guidance, it becomes a powerful source of motivation, leading to potentially remarkable outcomes.

The world desperately needs ambitious people.

The world desperately needs humble people.

> IN FACT, HUMILITY DOESN'T CRUSH AMBITION, IT PROVIDES THE NECESSARY GUARDRAILS TO PURSUE AMBITIOUS GOALS AND ASPIRATIONS APPROPRIATELY.

Humility and ambition aren't adversaries. They should co-exist in a delicate harmony. In fact, humility doesn't crush ambition, it provides the necessary guardrails to pursue ambitious goals and aspirations appropriately. Remarkable achievements, significant movements, and pivotal moments often occur because humble yet ambitious individuals dared to pursue them.

But for this to be true, we must let God be God instead of somehow trying to be God's surrogate. We could actually make a good theological argument that everyone suffers from this "God complex" problem, tracing back to the original temptation faced by Adam and Eve. They desired to be like God back then, just as we still do today.

- It's why we struggle to always be in control
- It's why we put up a false front and mask our vulnerabilities
- It's why we care about how many followers we have on social media and if they're glorifying us with likes and retweets.
- It's why we think we always know best, want to be the boss, feel capable of doing just about anything, believe we don't need to take a break, and think sleep is for lazy or dead people.

Again, when our heart is postured around pride it always leads to decline and an inevitable crash.

So, for all of us *Type I's* who want to be God, I have a little surprise for you.

Are you ready for it?

You sure?

Here it is: God is actually ... *humble.*

GOD IS HUMBLE

If you regularly read and believe the Bible, you can name some of God's primary characteristics. God is love. God is holy. God is all-knowing, all-powerful, and all-present. God is just and merciful. Yet, when we list His characteristics, there's one we tend to overlook.

God is humble.

Perhaps we miss it because it's counterintuitive. Maybe we find it challenging to grasp because it goes against our *Type I* instincts. Humility, the absence of pride and arrogance, seems paradoxical. Godly humility entails recognizing that nothing and no one is beneath us and that idea seems incompatible with our perception of God. Shouldn't God, who holds ultimate power, have the right to be prideful? Shouldn't He consider Himself superior to everything and everyone?

Yes. But remarkably, God is *humble*—very humble. In fact, one of the reasons Jesus came was to demonstrate God's humility to us. One of the most well-known examples of Jesus' humility happened the night before his crucifixion with His disciples, and once again, it includes our favorite *Type I*, Peter.

Here is the helpful context. In ancient times, it was customary for a servant to wash the feet of guests as they arrived at a home. People walked in sandals, and the roads were dirty. Their feet would become caked in dust, mud, and perhaps some animal droppings. Given the dusty and often dirty roads, this practice ensured cleanliness for communal meals, where people reclined with their feet exposed.

People actually ate their meals not sitting shoulder to shoulder, but *laying* head to feet, so clean feet were a must. A servant would bend down and carefully clean the disgusting debris from every guest who entered the home.

In John 13, we read that Jesus and his twelve disciples entered an upper room to have a meal together but there was a problem. There wasn't a servant to wash everyone's feet. Who would do it? Who would stoop so low as to wash everyone's disgusting, calloused feet? Volunteering to wash everyone's feet was seen as an act of extreme humility, indicating the lowest rank among the group. That's why ... *no one* volunteered. Certainly not Peter. If I had to put my money on one of the disciples, he would be my last bet.

As they settled in for the meal, the uncomfortable reality dawned upon them that their feet remained unwashed. The silence likely added to the awkwardness and odor of the moment.

Who do you think did it?

Only the most humble among them would be able to put their own comfort aside to serve the group. Of course, it was Jesus who actually made the move.

He got up, grabbed a basin, tied an apron around his waist, picked up a towel, and began the grimy job of cleaning each person's feet. Everyone's. Even Judas. Yes, that Judas who was already in the midst of betraying him. Through this humble act, Jesus demonstrated profound love and servitude to His disciples, humbling each one of them in receiving such undeserved care and attention.

Everyone except... you guessed it, Peter.

"He came to Simon Peter, who said to Him, "Lord, are you going to wash my feet?" Jesus replied, "You do not realize now what I am doing, but later you will understand."

"No," said Peter, "you shall never wash my feet." Jesus answered, "Unless I wash you, you have no part with me."

"Then, Lord," Simon Peter replied, "not just my feet but my hands and my head as well!" (John 13:6-9, NIV)

Peter, always good for entertainment, balks at the proposition of Jesus serving him. Why? He prioritized pride over humility. He couldn't fathom Jesus, whom he revered as their leader and teacher, performing a task typically reserved for servants. To Peter, allowing Jesus to wash his feet seemed degrading, beneath the dignity of someone as esteemed as Jesus.

While I imagine the other disciples sitting around speechless at Jesus' act of love and humility, I also envision them annoyed, palms on their foreheads, eyes rolled, wishing Peter would just shut up.

Per usual, Jesus gently quiets Peter. True to his impulsive nature, Peter's initial refusal quickly transformed into an exaggerated request for Jesus to wash his entire body. He moved from, "You can't wash my feet," to, "Wash all of me, Jesus!"

Jesus finishes washing everyone's feet and then gives them the proverbial why…

"I have set you an example that you should do as I have done for you. Very truly I tell you, no servant is greater than his master, nor is a messenger greater than the one who sent him. Now that you know these things, you will be blessed if you do them." (John 13:15-17, NIV).

Jesus explains that humility – believing that no one and nothing is beneath you, grabbing the towel, and doing whatever is necessary – is for *everyone.*

Humility says no person or task is beneath me.

Because God is humble, we need to be humble.

All of us.

Even us *Type I's* like Peter.

Peter definitely learned something that night. Because years later he reflectively wrote, *"Finally, all of you, be like-minded, be sympathetic, love one another, be compassionate and humble."* (1 Peter 3:8, NIV)

Peter went on to say, *"All of you, clothe yourselves with humility toward one another, because, "God opposes the proud but shows favor to the humble. Humble yourselves, therefore, under God's mighty hand, that he may lift you up in due time."* (1 Peter 5:5-6, NIV)

When Peter wrote, *"clothe yourselves with humility,"* I wonder if his mind wandered back to the evening as he re-lived Jesus literally tying humility around himself by donning a servant's apron, like someone who shows up early to wash everyone's feet.

God is humble.

WILL YOU BE HUMBLE?

Jesus set the example.

Peter and Paul call us to live a life of humility.

So let me ask the question again...

Are you willing?

Will you choose humility?

Will you allow pride or humility to lead the way? In your life, your job, your relationships, your places of influence, and your politics?

And before you think I'm only posing the questions to you, let me assure you, I'm not. These are filters all *Type I's*, including myself, must willingly ask themselves on a regular basis. I constantly live in the tension, wrestling to balance my desire for Godly ambition and His call to live a quiet life.

Humility doesn't come easily to me. I suspect it doesn't for you either. You're driven. You're getting stuff done. You're grabbing life by the throat as often as you can.

I wonder if it was ever hard for Jesus too. After spending all eternity in Heaven with His heavenly Father - Jesus spends thirty years in obscurity, basically fasting from praise, power, and position. Alicia Chole wonders how he must have wrestled with it in her book *40 Days of Decrease*. She writes,

> *"How must it have felt - knowing he had the power to heal - to have to walk past children suffering with leprosy? What would it have been like - knowing that his conception was miraculous - to be unable to defend his mother when others whispered about her*

past? And how agonizing would it be - when his word could one day raise the dead to life again - to stand by while those he loved (perhaps even Joseph his father) died?"[6]

JESUS CHOSE HUMILITY AND HE CALLS US
TO DO THE SAME, TO FAST FROM SELF.

Jesus chose humility and He calls us to do the same, to fast from self. It's easy to obsess over ourselves, to fill my life with me. Yet, Jesus emptied Himself and called you and me to do the same. It's only when we do, that we will begin to experience the fullness of God. Eugene Peterson writes:

"Christian spirituality is not about us. The great weakness of American spirituality is that it is all about us: fulfilling our potential, getting the blessings of God, expanding our influence, finding our gifts, getting a handle on principles by which we can get an edge over the competition. The more there is of the US, the less there is of GOD."[7]

He's so right. The more there is of us, the less there is of God. And when we choose humility, we empty ourselves of us so we can be filled with God.

So, what would it look like to choose humility? Here are a few ideas of how you might fast from self:

WHEN YOU SEE HUMILITY IN OTHER PEOPLE, IT'S BEAUTIFUL.
WHEN YOU HAVE TO LIVE THAT WAY, IT'S CHALLENGING.

1. DECIDE THAT NOTHING AND NO ONE IS BENEATH YOU.

When you see that attitude in other people, it's beautiful. When you have to live that way, it's challenging. But it's how we live beautiful, humble lives that look more like Jesus' life.

Nothing is beneath you—not cleaning up after the party, not scrubbing the toilet, not running the errands.

No one is beneath you. Not the intern. Not the person on the other side of the political aisle. Not the homeless person begging on the side of the road. Not the person who posts opposing comments on social media. No one.

2. RELY ON GOD AND OTHERS INSTEAD OF SELF.

Type I's prefer self-reliance. "I Got This" is our team motto. Someone asks, "Do you need help?" "No, I got this." "That box says it takes two people to lift." "No thanks. I got this."

"It's literally impossible for one person to do a teeter-totter. Do you want me to get on the other side?" "Nope, I got this."

We don't like help, from other people or God. While we may resort to prayer in moments of desperation, we generally maintain an attitude of self-sufficiency, believing we can handle any situation without assistance. "No God, you do your thing. I got this."

Too often this is my response. Maybe it's yours too. While appearing strong on the surface, this default toward self-reliance lacks humility. True strength, however, lies in acknowledging one's weaknesses and accepting help when needed.

Our self-reliance can also lead to seeing others around us as a threat. This will squash opportunities for collaboration and seeing others thrive fully in their God-given gifts and talents. Adam Grant calls this out,

> "Narcissistic leaders are threatened by talent. They want to be the smartest person in the room. Humble leaders are drawn to talent. They surround themselves with people who make them smarter."[8]

Self-reliance may feel more comfortable, but utter dependence is the truer friend for our souls. So our posture towards one another should be that of a humble servant. Or perhaps a better description would be... a quiet hero.

QUIET HEROS

As kids, we're drawn to heroes, figures we admire and seek to emulate. Sometimes, these heroes are real people, but often they're the stuff of legends and fiction. Growing up in the mid-1970s, there was the Six Million Dollar Man, Steve Austin. No, not the "Stone Cold" wrestler guy. This was the original Steve Austin—the one with bionic powers, robotic limbs, and an eye that could zoom in for a better view. He was awesome! I have fond memories of eagerly sitting in front of our large console television, which offered just three channels and tuning in each week to see what feats my hero would achieve. (If you're younger than 40, you might not be familiar with him. Feel free to google "The Six Million Dollar Man" trailer to get a glimpse.) I idolized Steve Austin and wanted to be just as cool as him.

Recently, someone revealed that they once revered Batman as their ultimate hero, until they realized that wearing a cape doesn't automatically transform someone into a savior of the night. However, there are individuals like Harriet Tubman, Gandhi, Mother Teresa, and even Fred Rogers who have become icons, serving as heroes to countless souls.

What's intriguing is that our perception of heroes evolves as we navigate through life. They transition from fictional figures with capes to real-life inspirations who specifically influence our teenage and young adult years. In my own experience, figures like

Tom Hinton and Doug Sites emerged as true early heroes. Though their names may not ring familiar, their lives spoke volumes, and their integrity and enthusiasm became the blueprint for my own life. Their impact began during my teenage years and continues to shape me to this day.

Then there are everyday heroes such as the neighbor I witnessed last week. Their hazard lights blinked as they parked along the curb, delivering a meal to someone who couldn't leave their home. These are the unsung heroes, quietly serving and "washing the feet" of others without seeking recognition.

> WE CELEBRATE HUMILITY AS A THEORY BUT
> HESITATE WHEN IT MUST BECOME REALITY.

Let's be honest: Foot-washing humility isn't effortless for any of us. We celebrate humility as a theory but hesitate when it must become reality, especially when it means washing the feet of those in our lives we deem difficult or undeserving.

People like:

- The Insensitive Coworker: You know, the one who lacks tact.
- The Opinionated Relative: The one who is aggressively adamant in all their opinions.
- The Often Forgotten: The one who often slips through the cracks
- The Aggressive Neighbor: The person who lives on your street who poses a challenge
- The Demanding Boss: The boss who makes relentless and often unreasonable demands.
- The Needy Friend: The friend who always seems to need more of you.

Marv and Marge are a couple of those quiet heroes. They attend the church I work at in Las Vegas. Over the years, I've gotten to know the pair who continue to inspire me with their humble, servant's hearts. Now in their eighties, they reflect the humility of

Christ in ways we all should emulate. It's easy to think that it's just a product of age and slower speed, but it resonates from a much deeper place from these two.

Despite their physical challenges, they raise their proverbial hands when they can fill a need or gap. I love to stand back by the sound booth and watch them specifically positioning themselves to experience the full wave of worship music that probably isn't their first choice and carries a few more DBs than they prefer. Yet they sway, arms lifted as high as they can, as they fully engage with Jesus.

The pair doesn't stop worshiping when the music and service ends. Instead, they position themselves in the coffee cafe area, mingling with others and specifically looking for those who are new or alone. Their humility is lived out throughout the week as they attend Bible study and various volunteer opportunities.

They see their role as bridging the gap. It's their way of washing feet. They want people to know and love Jesus. And while they welcome the opportunity to talk about Jesus, it's not required. Their quiet lives have a deep, far-reaching influence with countless ripple effects. They once may have embodied more of a *Type I* approach to life, but they now have settled into a quiet, but impactful existence.

In the midst of society's relentless noise and preoccupation with self, quiet heroes do persist, though they may be challenging to discern. We are called to embody heroism ourselves, mirroring Jesus by extending love to those closest to us, especially those who make it difficult. This involves a daily commitment to selflessly serving in a world tilted towards selfishness. Rather than succumbing to our natural self-centeredness, instead, we choose to embrace humility and take up the towel of service. In doing so, we leave a lasting impact.

WHEN OUR AMBITION IS DISCONNECTED FROM OUR HUMILITY, A CRASH IS INEVITABLE. WHEN OUR AMBITION IS BIRTHED FROM GOD AND BATHED IN THE WATERS OF HUMILITY, OUR IMPACT IS ENDLESS.

Let's be clear. When our ambition is disconnected from our humility, a crash is inevitable. But when our ambition is birthed from God and bathed in the waters of humility that mirror His, our impact is endless.

A beautiful prayer from early twentieth-century Spanish Catholic cardinal, Rafael Merry del Val y Zulueta, titled the "Litany of Humility," resonates deeply with me. Perhaps it will resonate with you too. It says, *"From the fear of being humiliated, deliver me, O Jesus,"*[9] The cardinal isn't requesting exemption from humiliation but rather the courage to confront our fear of it. Let this be our prayer. And then go ahead, let the Godly ambition loose in your life, but please, be humble and quiet about it.

KEY TAKEAWAYS AND DISCUSSION STARTERS:

. . . .

1. CONCEIT AND THE DESTRUCTIVE NATURE OF PRIDE: Whether categorized as a *Type I* or not, many individuals struggle with the desire to project an image of having everything under control. This often leads to an inappropriate swagger and a sense of elevated importance, especially for those in positions of authority or influence. Pride is a universal human issue, albeit more pronounced in *Type I's,* which leads to eventual downfall.

- How is it that you might be projecting an image of yourself that is not genuine?
- What are some ways you think that might help you learn to be more others-centered rather than only looking at yourself?

2. BALANCING AMBITION WITH HUMILITY: While ambition is considered a positive trait, it must be balanced with humility to avoid negative consequences. Humility serves as the necessary guardrail to prevent ambition from veering into arrogance or selfishness. Surrendering the desire to control and acknowledge God's sovereignty is crucial in maintaining this balance and avoiding the pitfalls of pride.

- What are some goals you are working toward that you need to bring God into?

3. EMULATING QUIET HEROES: The section concludes by celebrating the concept of "quiet heroes"—individuals who humbly serve others without seeking recognition or praise. These everyday heroes exemplify Christ-like humility through their selfless actions, whether delivering meals to the homebound, engaging with newcomers, or extending kindness to those in need. The narrative encourages readers to follow their example by embracing humility, serving others, and making a lasting impact in their communities.

- Name a quiet hero in your proximity. What traits of theirs do you hope to model in your own life?

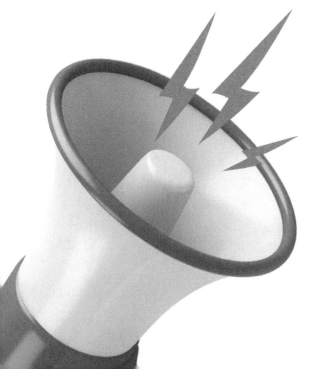

CHAPTER 8

COWARDICE

．．．．．．．．．．．

While I've never been much of a gamer, the pandemic shutdown in 2020 led me to try *NHL 20*. There were so many buttons and options, but I started to get the hang of it—well...sort of.

Then my son dropped by. Naturally, as fathers do with their grown sons, I initiated some friendly trash talk and challenged him to a virtual hockey match on the PS4. I was not confident. I was cocky.

He smiled but said nothing.

As the game began, it quickly became apparent that my confidence was unfounded. Within a matter of minutes, it was over. I was humiliated. My confidence was an illusion— words I knew I couldn't back up but hoped would somehow produce a victory. It didn't.

Whether you identify as a *Type I* or not, we've all likely experienced moments of overconfidence. It just comes more naturally for us *Type I's*. We assess the situation, evaluate the challenge, or anticipate a difficult conversation and think, "I've got this," just to be confronted with the truth that we don't.

Overconfidence and arrogance surrounding a video game are one thing. But when that perspective finds its way into our normal lives, we are setting ourselves up to not only be exposed but also to lose credibility, influence, and potentially our faith.

Confidence tends to come naturally for the *Type I* leader. In fact, a certain level of confidence is essential for driving change. Jon Lonsdale agrees, saying, *"You have to be a bit overconfident, and a big ego isn't always a bad thing. To change the world requires pushing really, really hard and believing you and your team know something others don't."[1]* But the gap between confidence and cowardice is perilously slim.

Peter's tendency toward overconfidence is well-documented. His affinity toward confidence was evident when he opened his mouth on the Mount of Transfiguration and again when he courageously stepped out of the boat onto the stormy waters. However, his most infamous moment of overconfidence led to his most significant moment of cowardice.

WHEN WHAT YOU'RE EXPECTING IS *NOT* WHAT YOU'RE EXPERIENCING

Let's revisit the evening before His crucifixion when Jesus gathered with His disciples for their final meal in a private room. Before they could begin eating, Jesus assumed the role of a servant, noticing that His disciples were already embracing their roles as future apostles and influential writers of the New Testament. As they sat down, Jesus humbly washed their feet. It's worth noting that Peter initially protested, demonstrating how our own confidence can sometimes hinder our ability to accept acts of service.

> *He came to Simon Peter, who said to him, "Lord, are you going to wash my feet?"*
> *Jesus replied, "You do not realize now what I am doing, but later you will understand."*
> *"No," said Peter, "you shall never wash my feet."*
> *Jesus answered, "Unless I wash you, you have no part with me."*
> *"Then, Lord," Simon Peter replied, "not just my feet but my hands and my head as well!" (John 13:6-9, NIV)*

Peter, again, sticks his foot in his mouth, this time while his foot is literally in Jesus' hands.

Once the awkward foot washing is over, the evening continues as everyone settles down to share the meal together. While they eat, Jesus begins to speak, giving what would be some final instructions to His disciples. He encourages them to demonstrate their love for Him by loving others. Jesus also hints at His looming departure, letting them know they cannot yet follow where He is going.

All of the disciples seem confused, and it's evident on their faces. Okay, they're very confused. Except, of course, for Peter. His confidence appears to be growing, and as everyone else quietly listens, his *Type I* kicks in.

Simon Peter asked him, "Lord, where are you going?"
Jesus replied, "Where I am going, you cannot follow now, but you will follow later."
Peter asked, "Lord, why can't I follow you now? I will lay down my life for you."
Then Jesus answered, "Will you really lay down your life for me? Very truly I tell you, before the rooster crows, you will disown me three times! (John 13:36-38, NIV)

Peter's bravado consistently goes before him. However, in this pivotal moment, Jesus locks eyes with Peter and delivers a solemn warning. He warns that Peter's strong conviction will soon be tested, his loyalty questioned, and his confidence crushed. Before the sun rises tomorrow, Jesus tells Peter, he will deny even knowing Him.

I can envision Peter's smirk in response.

"Me? You must be joking. I would never do such a thing."

It's a moment where his confidence, or rather, his overconfidence, is on full display.

Leaving the upper room behind, the scene transitions to the beautiful garden of Gethsemane. Jesus, accompanied by Peter, James, and John, retreats there to pray and prepare himself for what lies ahead. He knows what's coming. He carries the weight of upcoming events on His shoulders. Although Jesus is fully aware of what is to come, Peter and the other disciples are not. However, they have to sense the gravity of the situation.

Jesus asks them to pray, but as He pours out His heart in prayer, they just can't keep their eyes open and fall into a deep slumber. Though He wakes them up a few times, their eyes are too heavy. So while He sweats drops of blood in anguish, they are counting sheep, unaware of the turmoil approaching them.

Before long, the sounds of loud voices and the glow of torches shatter the quietness of the garden as a battalion of soldiers arrives to arrest Jesus. The angry mob emerges from the darkness, fired up, and prepared for violence. The flickering lights cast eerie shadows, revealing faces full of hostility, determined to end this rogue movement led by this carpenter-turned-Rabbi from Nazareth.

Jesus' disciples, who moments ago were snoring, suddenly find themselves wide-eyed and gripped by fear. They back up, paralyzed by indecision, doing nothing. Except... for Peter. True to form, he reacts impulsively. While the others back away, Peter steps in. His overconfidence leads him to act without thinking, a pattern of behavior based on reaction rather than deliberate response.

> ## THE AFFINITY TOWARD ACTION IS WHAT MAKES TYPE I'S BOTH VALUABLE AND VULNERABLE.

The affinity toward action is what makes *Type I's* both valuable and vulnerable. Driven by an unwavering supply of confidence, Peter instinctively taps into his inner gladiator, pulls his sword, and readies for battle. However, despite his boldness, a hint of cowardice seems to slip through the cracks as he takes action.

"Then Simon Peter, who had a sword, drew it and struck the high priest's servant, cutting off his right ear. (The servant's name was Malchus.)" (John 18:10, NIV).

Who arrived in the garden to arrest Jesus? Soldiers.

And who does Peter take on? *Not* one of the soldiers.

In the heat of the moment, Peter, armed with a sword, doesn't target the soldiers who have come to arrest Jesus, but rather the high priest's servant. It's a curious choice. The high priest is not a trained combatant; his servant is likely a young intern, probably even a teenager training for the priesthood. Despite this, Peter chooses the servant as the best target for his attack.

Looks brave.

But this wasn't courage at work.

It was cowardice disguised as confidence.

Jesus, the actual target of all this chaos, sees what has happened and responds in a way that likely caught Peter off guard with all his *Type I* confidence spilling out all over the place.

> *Jesus commanded Peter, "Put your sword away! Shall I not drink the cup the Father has given me?" Then the detachment of soldiers with its commander and the Jewish officials arrested Jesus. They bound him" (John 18:11-12, NIV).*

The gospel of Luke's account of this incident adds an element to this exchange. Jesus heals the man's ear. Peter amputates, and Jesus reattaches. The moment concludes with Jesus being led away, leaving the disciples stunned and reeling from the abrupt turn of events. But no one is impacted more than Peter. He thought he was stepping up, but instead, his confidence overstepped. There is always an element of overconfidence that stems from forgetting where any and all confidence should originate from.

> ## CONFIDENCE MISPLACED WILL CAUSE US TO FALL SHORT OF THE DESTINATION GOD INTENDED FOR US.

Paul reminds us where our confidence should begin and end: *"That he who began a good work in you will carry it on to completion until the day of Christ Jesus" (Philippians 1:6, NIV).* Confidence misplaced will cause us to fall short of the destination God intended for us.

If you want to see this principle in action, sign up for a marathon. Yes, go ahead, and sign up for 26.2 miles of grueling challenge and brutality. There are several reasons why only a small percentage of the earth's population ever crosses the finish line of a marathon. For one, it's just dumb. Secondly, it demands weeks and months of rigorous training, mostly in isolation, to prepare your body for race day. And third, it will challenge your confidence and expose your doubts.

It's often said that a marathon is essentially a 20-mile warm-up followed by a grueling six-mile finish. This is not wrong. If an individual has trained appropriately, the first twenty miles will typically be a grind but manageable. In fact, a runner will likely feel pretty good about themselves for the first 18-20 miles. That's an illusion.

In 2014, I signed up for my first marathon in San Diego. After months of training and preparation, I toed the start line with 10,000 fellow runners, overflowing with confidence. With each passing mile, my confidence only increased, especially as the crowd of runners began to thin out after the first ten miles. I was cruising effortlessly, feeling good, and wondering what the big deal was about running a marathon.

In fact, I had already envisioned myself completing my first marathon in under four hours, a standard benchmark for average runners, and relishing the thrill of wearing that medal around my neck. I was already preparing for everyone at breakfast the next morning who would see my medal and ask, "Did you just run a marathon?"

"Of course, " I would respond confidently, "and actually it was surprisingly easy."

My wife and I had already planned a meeting spot along the course. She would be meeting me along the route as I approached mile nineteen so I was looking forward to seeing her, exchanging high fives, and letting her know that I was killing it. In fact, that's exactly what I did. As I approached, I veered towards the spectator rope, greeted her with a quick kiss on the cheek, and proudly let her know how great I felt. She just smiled and said, "I'll see you in a few minutes at the finish line." I gave her a thumbs up and headed out to complete my victory tour towards the finish line.

A few minutes later something changed. It wasn't immediate. It slowly started to creep in. What was it? Pain. Exhaustion. Cramps. And as the discomfort crept in, my confidence slowly crawled away. By the time I reached a challenging uphill section with only three miles remaining, I was running on empty. And I wasn't alone. A carnage of runners was all around me as they slowed down, stopped, and some even sat down by the side of the road, unable to continue.

All of the cockiness I felt back at mile ten had vanished. The thumbs up to my wife at mile nineteen was a distant memory. I had hit the wall, the physical and psychological reality where your mind and your body seem to refuse to move forward anymore. Some runners can push through it. Others tap out.

The harsh reality of how hard it would be to finish strong slapped me in the face. I managed to walk, limp, and almost crawl to the finish line. I finished. I got a medal. However, the blow to my confidence was a brutal lesson for this *Type I*. In fact, it was a necessary one.

Peter was about to hit the wall as well. Except in his case, it wasn't just an arbitrary physical barrier in an athletic event; it was a moment that would haunt him for the rest of his life. His expectations lay shattered, and his confidence was severely shaken. His experience of the past few hours made him question everything he had experienced over the past three years walking alongside Jesus.

Perhaps Peter hoped that the violent scene in the garden would mark the beginning of a violent uprising establishing Jesus as king with absolute authority and power on earth, and Peter alongside him. Despite everything Jesus had taught—all the turn the other cheek, walk the extra mile stuff—Peter's perception of what a Messiah would bring was still skewed. He struggled to accept that all of this kingdom talk would have nothing to do with the defeat of Rome. His dreams and expectations had been dashed.

At that moment, Peter lost all hope and ran.

The narrative of Jesus' life, as depicted in Mark's gospel,

is attributed to Mark himself, but the content came from Peter's own experience. One can imagine Peter sitting with Mark towards the end of his life, recounting every detail of his journey following Jesus. Peter doesn't sugarcoat the truth or details. His candor and honesty in presenting the good, the bad, and the ugly aspects of his experiences are admirable.

This next passage definitely falls into the category of the ugly. I even wonder if Mark asked Peter, "Are you sure you want to document this for the future?" If so, Peter must have answered, "Yes, because it's what happened and it's important for others who will find themselves in a similar moment." It would have been easy for Peter to omit this part of his story, purposefully erasing it from history. Yet, he chose not to, demonstrating a level of humility that transcended his own interests.

And so, Mark recorded what happened next which was simply, *"Everyone deserted him (Jesus) and fled" (Mark 14:50, NIV).*

As they witnessed Jesus being led away to face trial, and with the reality of His execution weighing heavy, they must have felt that all hope was lost. All of the confidence they had gained from witnessing Jesus heal the sick, raise the dead, and challenge the religious authorities of their time faded. In their eyes, Jesus no longer appeared to be the long-awaited Messiah, nor the promised King. The kingdom Jesus spoke of seemed like a distant dream that would never materialize. It was over. Their expectations now felt like a figment of their imagination.

Peter found himself in a puzzling and confusing mindset because what he was EXPERIENCING didn't align with what he was EXPECTING.

Like Peter, our faith can deteriorate when our situations deviate from what we anticipate. We might start doubting God and imagining the worst possible outcomes during our darkest times. In such moments, fear can overpower our faith, leading to actions driven by cowardice.

> OUR FAITH CAN DETERIORATE WHEN OUR SITUATIONS DEVIATE FROM WHAT WE ANTICIPATE.

When life veers off course from our expectations, it can be draining. We've talked about how individual *Type I's* tend to grapple with control issues. When circumstances spiral beyond our influence and outcomes become unclear, exhaustion and frustration creep in. Have you ever encountered this feeling?

When life doesn't conform to your plans, it leaves you weary—tired of waiting, tired of striving, tired of feeling disappointed by others, tired of falling short, tired of unrealized hopes. In these moments, we come face to face with a truth articulated by legendary Army general George S. Patton to his troops during World War II in 1944: "Fatigue turns us all into cowards."[2]

> IN THE MIDST OF FATIGUE, WE OFTEN
> EXCHANGE OUR FAITH FOR FEAR.

In the midst of fatigue, we often exchange our faith, which appears to have let us down, for fear. Fear transforms us into fortune tellers, confident in predicting what lies ahead and what doesn't. We might convince ourselves that we're trapped in the present moment, that change is impossible, or that any change will only bring chaos. The future seems out of control, you are confused, and God's plan is difficult to discern. Your *Type I* begins to spiral.

I recall a season early in my pastoral career when my wife and I felt called to establish a new church in Las Vegas. The city was booming, the need was great, and our love for our community was strong. It resonated deeply with all the *Type I* characteristics within me. So we did it.

It was great.

It was a grind.

It was exhilarating.

It was exhausting.

If you have ever taken on the monumental task of being

entrepreneurial, you know that starting anything new requires resilience and realism. Planting a church falls squarely into this category—it demands perseverance in the demands of the daily slog and belief in the vision of a better tomorrow. It means navigating both the eternal calling and the practical realities of day-to-day survival. From shepherding the congregation to managing finances and caring for our own family, as a *Type I*, it proved to be the most demanding and stretching season of my life.

By the seventh year, my faith was wavering, and my energy was wearing thin. It had been a year marked by significant leaps of faith. The church had taken on the strenuous journey of securing land, fundraising, and building its first permanent facility. It involved months of countless meetings, negotiations with contractors and banks, and a barrage of decisions, many of which were largely mine to make. Of course, my *Type I* kicked in and there were aspects of those challenges that I thrived in. But inside I was losing steam.

One day during the early morning hours, as the project neared its completion, I found myself alone in the building. My daughter Ashlee kept herself occupied by zooming around the concrete floors in her Heely shoes, which doubled as skates. However, I was NOT entertained. With a rented paint sprayer in hand, I moved back and forth tirelessly, alternating between working on and off a ladder, desperately trying to finish painting the interior walls of our new church home before the cabinetry arrived the next day.

I was covered in paint.

I was exhausted.

I was alone.

It was dark. Not just outside, but also inside my soul.

As I left in the wee hours of the morning, the painting finished, something else felt finished. My heart. I didn't know it then, but what was supposed to be a beginning actually signaled the beginning of the end.

Construction concluded over the next few weeks, and we celebrated our first weekend gathering as a church family in our new home. It marked the culmination of a grueling seven-year journey, filled with the highs and lows typical of any startup venture. We definitely celebrated. We applauded. We laughed. We prayed. It was a good day.

However, the toll of relentless grinding year after year was catching up to me. Spiritually drained and emotionally vulnerable, the very building we were celebrating had already begun to feel like a burden. Ironically, the finish line of the building's completion would also become a personal finish line.

It didn't take long for reality to hit home. In the midst of the celebration, an influential couple who had played a significant role in completing our project pulled me aside in the lobby. I wondered if they were poised to generously offer more help. Perhaps they had some strong words of encouragement I desperately needed at that moment. My depleted soul was ready for them to refill me.

"We just wanted you to know how incredible this moment is," they said. I shook my head in agreement. I was so excited about what I knew was coming. They continued, "And we have so loved being a part of and watching this, but..." they paused, apparently for dramatic effect, "...we wanted you to know that this is our last day at the church. We told ourselves we would see the church into the building and then we'd be done. So, we just wanted to let you know. We love you and will be praying for the church."

I stood there, stunned and speechless. I mumbled something incoherent, and they walked away—simply walked away.

Of course, I'm definitely not Jesus, but flashback to the moment in the garden captured by Mark when he said, they all ran and fled. That's what this moment felt like.

That was the end.

I was done.

That was NOT what I was expecting.

So what do you do when what you're expecting is not what you're experiencing?

Later in his life, Peter would reflect on the significant role of humility during such difficult times, when our expectations remain unmet and anxiety reaches its peak. He wrote:

"Humble yourselves, therefore, under God's mighty hand, that he may lift you up in due time. Cast all your anxiety on him because he cares for you." (1 Peter 5:6-7, NIV)

We've already talked about humility's key role in every *Type I's* life. In those moments when God's actions don't align with our desires, or when we realize we haven't followed God's desires, humility becomes essential. Peter urges us to *humble ourselves*.

To be humble means I must:
- Admit I may not have the best perspective.
- Concede that I don't have the entire story.
- Acknowledge it's possible I'm not as smart and all-knowing as I believe I am.

Peter says to humble yourself *under God's mighty hand*. I believe that means:
- God does have the best perspective.
- God knows the entire story including our part in it.
- God is smarter and all-knowing in ways I am not.

Peter assures us that if we humble ourselves, God *will lift you up in His perfect timing*. Your current circumstances may not be what you want. God may not be doing what you expect right now. But even still, you can trust Him. While there is so much we don't understand, if we know Jesus, we know He is trustworthy even in the midst of uncertainty. We can unload all our worries onto Him because He genuinely cares for us. Our confidence needs to shift from self-confidence to God-confidence. Surrendering our lives and will to Him, without holding back, allows us to have full confidence that He will uplift us at the right moment.

OUR CONFIDENCE NEEDS TO SHIFT FROM
SELF-CONFIDENCE TO GOD-CONFIDENCE.

That is a great meme or quick social post, isn't it? Easy to post and quote, but much harder to actually do. I need this reminder too. Although the example I just shared happened almost two decades ago, it could easily happen again if I allow my *Type I* desires to run wild. To give into that strong need to be in charge, to set my own expectations of how, when, and where God will show up will quickly take over. That's my default rather than humbly allowing God to use the *Type I* wiring He instilled in me for His glory. My glory is much easier to seek than God's.

Peter's perspective in his later letter reflects a mature understanding of humility, but that wasn't his mindset the night before Jesus' crucifixion. It wasn't where he was when Jesus was arrested and everyone else fled. Peter's confidence waned rapidly in those unexpected and disturbing events. He found himself grappling with doubt and uncertainty, much like we often do when our experiences deviate from our expectations. And that grappling led him into the fire.

FORGED BY FIRE

While others fled, Peter at least followed. Although humiliated in the garden, curiosity compelled him to keep an eye on the unfolding events of that night from a reasonable distance. Eventually, he found himself in a dimly lit courtyard, huddled next to a small fire. With his head bowed, avoiding eye contact, he sought to remain anonymous, anxiously awaiting the outcome of Jesus' fate.

Like a celebrity trying to stay incognito, Peter pulls his figurative hat down and hides behind the dark glasses of his loyalty. His hope is to watch, but not to be identified as someone associated with Jesus. His *Type I* confidence is now at an all-time low. Not long before his cover is blown, a servant girl spots Peter, recognizes him, and calls him out.

"You were with Him," she exclaims confidently. His weak, but irritated response? *"I am not"* (John 18:17, NIV).

His confidence is now fully replaced by cowardice.

The floodgates of recognition open wide. Some others in the courtyard ask, *'You aren't one of his disciples too, are you?' He denied it, saying, 'I am not'"* (John 18:25, NIV).

Then comes the personal blow. Peter's previous moment of ear hacking comes back to haunt him as...*"One of the high priest's servants, a relative of the man whose ear Peter had cut off, challenged him, 'Didn't I see you with him in the garden?' Again Peter denied it."* (John 18:26-27, NIV).

It's interesting how Peter's account, as relayed through Mark, omits a crucial detail included by another biographer of Jesus. Matthew provides additional insight into Peter's response to the third question, revealing, *"Then he began to call down curses, and he swore to them, 'I don't know the man!'"* (Matthew 26:74, NIV).

Wow! The shift in Peter's demeanor is swift. At this point, fear, anxiety, and uncertainty have completely replaced Peter's previous faith and confidence. The same faith that prompted him to defend Jesus just a few hours earlier has now evaporated. He finds himself in a full-faith meltdown and self-preservation mode.

Then, just as Jesus predicted, *"a rooster crowed and Peter remembered the word Jesus had spoken: "Before the rooster crows, you will disown me three times." And he went outside and wept bitterly"* (John 18:74-75, NIV).

Peter is completely broken. He is a failure.

You've been there. I know you have. Like Peter, feeling like a failure as you sat by the fire of your circumstances, your faith melting in the heat.

After completing our building project, I found myself in a similar full-faith meltdown. The sheer exhaustion coupled with the disappointment of that couple leaving left me, even as a *Type I*, feeling utterly defeated. Instead of celebrating the accomplishment and how incredibly God had worked, I was done. I couldn't comprehend how God could lead me this far only to abandon me.

My next move wasn't courageous; it was cowardly. I will unpack it more in the next chapter, but suffice it to say, I tapped out.

Reflecting on that season, I realize now that I had no idea what God was truly orchestrating. And I think the same is true of Peter. As he sat by the fire, shattered by his failure and denial, Peter was oblivious to God's larger plan or how this pivotal moment would continue to mold him.

A few years back, our church held a leadership conference. The theme was *Forged*. I felt honored when they asked me to speak for one of the sessions, but I confess I had no clue what the word "forged" meant. It sounded impressive, but I feared being exposed once I started talking. So, I did what any sensible person would do—I turned to my trusty friends, Google and YouTube.

First, I needed a definition. I quickly discovered that forged is a verb meaning *"to form (something, such as metal) by heating and hammering."*[3]

Imagine a small pizza oven that can get ridiculously hot - hotter than a scorching July afternoon in Vegas, which is saying something. A blacksmith places the raw material, known as billets, into the forging furnace, allowing the intense heat to work its magic on the material. Remove it prematurely, before the heat has rendered it pliable, and the ensuing hammering process will result in damage rather than reshaping. However, if the material remains in the furnace until it reaches the optimal temperature, it will gradually take on a reddish-orange hue. It is at this ideal temperature, it will be placed on an anvil, where it can be skillfully formed into a usable object.

As the iron begins to cool, its color shifts and darkens, an indicator that to be molded further, it must be returned to the fire to regain its red-hot, pliable state. The blacksmith then continues the process with more pounding, squeezing, twisting, and molding until the iron gradually takes on the desired form, becoming a useful end product.

It's truly a remarkable process, but it can only occur through applying intense heat and pressure. Let that resonate with you for a moment. Perhaps for another moment.

As children, we're taught to fear fire.

As adults, we're conditioned to avoid fiery circumstances.

As Christ's followers, fire may be our greatest faith ally.

While we typically view fire as destructive, God often employs it to forge a deeply formed character and faith within us. Throughout Scripture, we see examples of God's use of fire:

- God spoke to Moses through a burning bush, revealing his presence and calling.
- God led His people out of Egypt by a pillar of fire during the darkness of night, guiding and protecting them.
- God sent a miracle of fire as a response from heaven to consume Elijah's water-soaked sacrifice, demonstrating His power and authority.
- God used tongues of fire to empower and equip the early church, preparing them to spread the gospel to the ends of the earth.

And it was next to a fire that God chose to forge Peter.

In each instance, fire symbolizes God's presence, power, and transformative work in the lives of His people. Instead of fearing fiery trials, we can actually embrace them as opportunities for God to shape us.

Earlier, Peter stood up, first among the disciples, to boldly express his convictions about Jesus: *"You are the Christ, the Son of the living God"* (Matthew 16:16, NIV). I will die for you" (John 13:37, NIV).

Perhaps you too have convictions you've proclaimed about and to Jesus. But when those convictions come under fire, it can be a challenging and unsettling experience. Will those moments become failure points or forging points?

Peter melted in the heat of the moment.

It had all the makings of a permanent failure.

But it was more than that. There is more to the story.

Peter's failure would be a catalyst for the deepening of his conviction. He put himself in the fire, but God – who causes everything to work together for the good of those who love him and are called according to his purpose – took the opportunity to forge Peter into something he never would have been otherwise. He would not have been prepared for the future leadership and purpose God had for him.

Who better to tell people about God's profound grace than someone who had failed God so profoundly? Who better than someone who had so deeply experienced the greatest healing force in the universe, God's unconditional love?

Peter didn't realize that at the moment. That night in the courtyard, as he denied Jesus and wept bitterly, it felt like the worst moment of his life, which it was. Yet paradoxically, it would also become the most formative.

We see this again as he fully understands the power of fire when he writes,

"In all this, you greatly rejoice, though now for a little while you may have had to suffer grief in all kinds of trials. These have come so that the proven genuineness of your faith—of greater worth than gold, which perishes even though refined by fire—may result in praise, glory, and honor when Jesus Christ is revealed." (1 Peter 1:6-7, NIV)

Having emerged from the heat of forging, Peter wanted to assure all of us, especially his fellow *Type I's*, that God's love is available to us when we are going through the fire.

Peter is leaning in, looking at us, and calmly saying, "I get it. I understand. I've walked that path. I remember when my future seemed bleak, when I, once resolute, faltered into cowardice. I lost faith, deserted my beliefs, and felt abandoned by God. But He never left my side. In those moments, He was shaping me. Just as He desires to shape you. He does so by refining your faith...in the midst of trials. Though it may feel like you're melting, you're actually being molded into something stronger."

AT THE CROSSROADS

In moments of faltering courage, we stand at a crossroads, confronted with a choice. It was precisely at this crossroads that Peter found himself as he stumbled out of that courtyard and into the shadows. His choice? To wander away. To wander back. To resist forging and remain stuck. His confidence, shaken to its core, had brought him to this pivotal moment. He had journeyed alongside Jesus, taking bold steps of faith even in the face of overwhelming fear. But this moment was different. He stood at the edge, peering into an uncertain future, teetering on the brink of his destiny. Was he going to go forward or lean into the difficult way back?

I was in my twenties on my first visit to New York City when I found myself at a precipice of confidence. The Statue of Liberty is an amazing monument both visually and for what she represents. I made the trek out to Liberty Island, just a short ferry ride from lower Manhattan, and stared up at this colossal statue. After walking in circles a few times, I ventured inside and discovered that a ticket could be purchased to climb the stairs to the crown. I must have lost my mind at that moment because I quickly purchased a ticket and followed the crowd onto the narrow, ancient staircase that wound up out of sight.

I know you've been anxiously waiting for another confession so here goes... I am shamelessly scared of heights. Like a small step stool around the house is the extent of my comfort climbing anything. Now I started my ascent up the 354 steps toward the crown. Did I mention it was dark? Very dark. People in front of me moved slowly. People behind me gently urged me forward. I had made a drastic error in judgment that there was no turning back from.

Somehow, I finally reached the small, cave-like opening where a few small windows in the crown allowed me to catch a glimpse of the Manhattan skyline for a moment or two. I paused, leaned over, took a look, and backed away. That was it.

Except it wasn't. The climb was terrifying, but I quickly realized what lay before me. The descent. Actually, before the descent was a decision. Would I allow my fear to take over to the point where they would have to call the FDNY to carry me down? Or would I take a deep breath, embracing the forging that was happening, and make my way back down, one step at a time? It's a choice that each of us must make when the fire of our circumstances is burning hot. *Type I's* will not and cannot escape these moments. Our default tendency to innovate, instigate, and initiate will also set us up for moments when we fail badly, lose our confidence, and act cowardly. Will we shrink back in those moments?

Or will we be forged and formed to fight our way forward? The choice is yours.

And no, I didn't have to be carried down from Lady Liberty's crown. I made it on my own, sweating profusely and maybe swearing silently the entire time because the way back can be even more terrifying. As we are about to see.

KEY TAKEAWAYS AND DISCUSSION STARTERS:

. . . .

1. BEWARE OF OVERCONFIDENCE: There is danger in overconfidence, especially in situations where one's abilities or understanding may be limited. Whether it's in a video game or real-life scenarios, overconfidence can lead to humiliation, loss of credibility, and ultimately failure.

- What scenario in your everyday life makes you feel overconfident? Do you desire to feel this way in other scenarios you might not understand completely?

2. MISPLACED EXPECTATIONS LEAD TO DISILLUSIONMENT: When what we expect does not align with our experiences, it can lead to disillusionment, doubt, and fear. This can cause us to act out of character and make decisions we later regret.

- Can you think of a time when your expectations did not match your experience? How did that affect you? What was your reaction to this experience?

3. CHOOSING FORWARD OR BACKWARD: When confronted with the consequences of failure and fear, individuals must either move forward or retreat. Like Peter stumbling out of the courtyard, we must decide whether to embrace the forging process, allowing our faith to be molded in the fire of adversity, or to remain stuck in cowardice and fear. Moving forward may be daunting, but it leads to growth and transformation while retreating only prolongs the struggle.

- How is it that God might be calling you to move forward? What does it look like for you to do so with confidence?
- God calls us out of self-assurance and into reliance on Him. What situation in your life do you think it might be good to allow God to be part of?

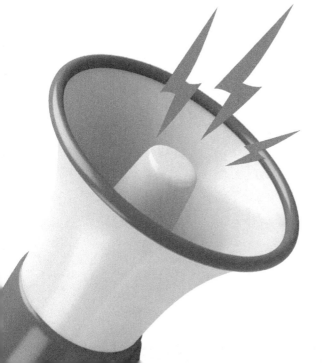

CHAPTER 9

COMEBACK

. . . .

LIVING IN 1985

It's been said that you can't go back again. It's an old and familiar cliché. I'm not sure of its origin or even its true meaning. But I do know this:

You can go back again.

But it probably won't end well.

Remember the couple who'd delivered that gut-punching announcement that they were leaving now that the church building project was complete? Well, within two weeks of their departure, two significant events occurred that shook what was left of my confidence and dramatically altered the trajectory of my life.

First, our church faced a serious financial crunch. To label it a mere "tightening" would be a gross understatement; it was a full-blown crisis. The additional cost of a new facility combined with some aggressive *Type I* growth initiatives I kicked off, emptied any margin in our resources. In fact, within a few weeks, it had become impossible to pay all the bills and still cover payroll. As a result, I chose to make the painful decision to forego my own paycheck. However, let me dispel any notion of this being a noble act of leadership; it was not. It was a necessity, not a choice. My attitude was not one of humility and confidence, but rather it triggered emotions in me that started a downward spiral. The financial tightening was also tough on my young family.

In the midst of this crisis, a ray of hope pierced through the darkness in the form of a phone call from an old friend in ministry. This friend had recently assumed the role of lead pastor at a thriving, large church just outside Seattle. We had attended seminary together and became good friends when we worked as youth pastors at this suburban church. Back then, he led a motley crew of young, ambitious leaders—mostly *Type I's*—each driven by a blend of passion, dedication, and a shared love for the teenagers we served.

None of us really knew what we were doing, but we had a lethal combination of zeal, loyalty, long nights, empty pizza boxes, and endless cups of coffee. It was a time of growth, camaraderie, and unforgettable memories shaped by our deep love for teenagers and our belief that connecting them with Christ would have an eternal and significant influence on their lives. It was a formative and fun time for all of us.

What initially seemed like a random call many years later turned out to hold far more significance than I could have imagined. My friend's church was flourishing, with over a thousand members riding a wave of tremendous momentum. (If you're a non-church reader, one thousand members is a large church.) He reached out to me under the genuine premise of a "curiosity call," expressing interest in my well-being and hoping I might consider joining his team.

Given my own state of turmoil, I was naturally interested. That initial casual conversation led to follow-up calls, which eventually led to a very compelling job offer. However, beneath the surface, a deeper narrative was unfolding. My friend had recently experienced the loss of his closest staff member amidst messy circumstances, leaving him feeling battered, confused, and adrift. He was seeking individuals he could rely on, people he could trust to navigate the challenges ahead.

In truth, we were both grappling with our own emotional trauma and longing to surround ourselves with a circle of trusted allies. It's a common trait among *Type I's* to seek solace in the company of others like themselves during times of crisis. We look to surround ourselves with others who can reassure, remove doubt, and help us forge our way forward.

Here's what I knew with certainty: if I were to accept his job offer, I would undergo a dramatic transformation from a struggling church planter to an executive pastor, complete with a prestigious office, expense account, personal assistant, and shiny new Mac laptop. Additionally, I would be entrusted with leading a sizable staff—an idea that resonated deeply with my *Type I* traits. The need to lead large, the need to lead loud, the need to seemingly make a significant impact every single day, was intoxicating. I was eager to leave behind my current struggles and step into the role of the hero.

It felt ... comfortable.

It felt... convenient.

> WHEN TWO LOST PEOPLE COLLIDE IN THE MIDST OF THEIR OWN DARK CIRCUMSTANCES, IT RARELY BRINGS COMFORT. MORE OFTEN, IT'S CATASTROPHIC.

I wasn't wise enough at that moment to recognize that when two lost people collide in the midst of their own dark circumstances, it rarely brings comfort. More often, it's catastrophic.

This was about to be catastrophic.

I know what you're thinking. *Why didn't you just stay in Vegas and press on, no matter how tough it might have been? How bad could it have been? Come on Lee. This is the moment when the Type I in you digs in, prays harder, and fights harder. This is when you look in the mirror, give yourself a pep talk, and get after it. This is precisely the kind of situation where all that Type I mentality should kick in.*

And you're right. I agree wholeheartedly. But the truth is, I simply didn't have the strength to keep moving forward. I was utterly exhausted and emotionally drained. The prospect of forging ahead seemed daunting and overwhelming. I couldn't even fathom it. Eventually, someone (my therapist, to be exact, whom I began seeing weekly to sort through all of this - more on that in a moment) would describe my decision to leave Las Vegas and return to Seattle as my "parachute moment." It was the moment when I decided to pull the ripcord, slip back into what I knew felt comfortable, and bail out on my calling even if it meant landing in an uncertain, less-than-ideal situation.

That's exactly what I did. I pulled the ripcord.

Without hesitation, I made the call, accepted the lucrative offer, and spun the appropriate "churchy" explanations when asked about the pending move.

A few weeks later, we said goodbye to our beloved church family and the community we loved, as our family headed to Seattle. As the bright lights of Vegas faded in the rearview mirror, I found some solace in the belief that Seattle held the key to everything I believed I was missing. Rest would replace my sleepless nights and every anxiety that had plagued me for years would finally dissipate.

I was wrong.

BACK OR BACKWARD

You probably know this, but parachuting out of your problem zone rarely works. Whenever we metaphorically pull the ripcord, hoping for a smooth transition to a more comfortable life, the reality often falls short of our expectations. This is especially true when we attempt to circle back to a life we are no longer called to and is not God's current plan for us. Instead of a soft landing, we find ourselves exchanging one set of challenges for another. This was certainly the case for me. There was no blissful place awaiting me in my new circumstances; instead, all my stress and exhaustion seemed to hitch a ride in the moving truck alongside our belongings, eagerly anticipating my arrival in the new location. While new surroundings can be refreshing, they rarely address our deeper issues of dysfunction or seasons of spiritual drought.

Within weeks of our arrival in Seattle, a heavy gray cloud settled over me, matching the dreary skies synonymous with the Pacific Northwest. A sense of unease began to gnaw at me, growing stronger with each passing day. What I had initially interpreted as progress now felt like a regression—a step backward rather than forward.

It wasn't a good feeling. It's one many of us grapple with.

We often head backward when moving forward in life seems too difficult, reflecting longingly into the rearview mirror of our lives, yearning to return to a particularly comfortable place or a time that now seems more ideal than it was. We idealize moments and phases of our lives but fail to realize we are at our best when moving forward, not stuck gazing backward at what is behind. Living in the rearview mirror is a sad and frustrating place to live. It is a poor reflection of reality and hinders our journey because it superimposes itself over the true destination that awaits us.

Can you relate? Have you ever found yourself there? Maybe you're experiencing it at this very moment. Think back to when the uncertainty of the future felt so overwhelming that you retreated into the comfort of the past. Where do you want to go? Perhaps you're already there, struggling to break free. You made the move backward and despite your best efforts, that nagging feeling of being stuck persists deep within you.

- You found yourself slipping back into an old relationship—the one you had once been relieved to end—simply because the prospect of finding a new one felt too daunting.
- You opted to remain in a job or career path you knew wasn't fulfilling simply because its familiarity seemed safer than venturing into an uncertain future.
- You chose to coast along in your current endeavors, fully aware that it would yield subpar results because you lacked the energy to make the difficult decisions required to pursue greater success.
- During a rough patch, you reverted to old patterns, behaviors, and activities, even though they were less fulfilling or purposeful, simply because they offered a sense of comfort and familiarity.
- Or it could be that you tried to do something bold, something that was exactly what your *Type I* was wired to do, but you crashed and burned, so your response was to retreat to the old and the familiar, which felt safe.

Many of us can relate to this pattern—we retreat to what we know, even if it means stepping back from our aspirations or potential for growth. That's what I did, and that's actually what Peter did…He headed back.

WHAT AM I DOING HERE?

Let's revisit the moment when Jesus called Peter while he was fishing. Peter was fully engaged in running the family business, which consisted of fishing the waters of the Sea of Galilee alongside his brother under the watchful eye of their father.

Whether it's a donut shop or an auto repair shop, managing a family business is a serious responsibility. Peter accepted this reality, knowing he would one day inherit and continue the fishing tradition. Raised in the small village nestled beside the sea he fished, Peter's mornings always began at the crack of dawn as he accompanied his father and brother to the water's edge, starting the day's work.

The boat might have needed repairs, and the nets required preparation—certainly not tasks a young boy would love to be doing in the early hours of the morning. While a few extra minutes of sleep would have been awesome, there was no room for that in the world of running a family fishing business, and Peter was a key part of that family.

My childhood echoed Peter's in many ways, as my family also owned a business. My father dedicated his life to covering the desert landscape of our hometown, Tucson, Arizona, with concrete. He tackled everything, from sidewalks and driveways to foundations and pool decks.

Which meant, I did it all as well.

Whether I wanted to be or not.

While other kids soaked up the sun by the pool during summer break, I found myself riding shotgun in my dad's worn-out 1972 Chevy pickup, surrounded by concrete trowels and rusty shovels bouncing around in the bed. We were that pickup you didn't want to be stuck behind on the freeway, complete with an 8-track tape player blaring classic country tunes by legends like Merle Haggard and Charley Pride.

I was young, but I wasn't stupid. I quickly learned the art of positioning myself strategically at each day's worksite. In the scorching Arizona desert, where temperatures soared well over 100°F, the most coveted spot was undoubtedly tool washing duty. Tasked with removing wet concrete from the tools before the sun could bake it onto the metal, I embraced the responsibility.

The true perk of this role? The accompanying water hose. No matter how oppressive the heat, the water flowing from that precious hose was always refreshingly ice cold. Passionately, I focused the hose onto the tools, allowing the glorious overspray to consistently cool me down in the sweltering heat.

I can't help but wonder if Peter ever sought solace in the shallow waters, enjoying the cool refreshing of the lake's gentle waves as the sun slowly rose in the sky. Perhaps his father would throw an occasional proud glance in his direction, proud of his son's strong work ethic, confident that the family legacy and livelihood would be in good hands in the future.

I also wonder if Peter ever dared to entertain aspirations of a different life—a life that felt more significant, more expansive. Could it be that the fiery spirit of a *Type I* nature simmered deep within his soul, yearning to break free even as he toiled knee-deep in the water alongside his family? If so, Peter must have felt deep down that those dreams could never be more than just dreams. He seemed destined to fish, born to be the keeper of the family business.

But then it happened.

The collision.

Peter lets Jesus borrow his boat for a speaking engagement. Jesus then takes it to the next level by inviting himself fishing. The fish fill the previously empty nets. Peter realizes this is a crucial moment and freaks out. Jesus calmly invites Peter to leave the life he was leading and become a different kind of fisherman. Peter leaves the family business. End of story.

He would spend the next three years alongside Jesus, seeing the miraculous happen and gaining an understanding of life through the lens of God's kingdom. There would be no turning back. That day everything changed and, of course, Peter would never go back to fishing.

Ever.

Except...

In our previous chapter, we witnessed Peter, who had seen Jesus regularly perform miracles, passionately professing his undying allegiance and loyalty to Him, only to suddenly deny even knowing Him when the pressure was on. He then stood idly by as Jesus was arrested, beaten, falsely accused, and ultimately sentenced to death. Every characteristic that typically defined Peter as a leader and influencer seemed to be absent on that fateful night.

Part of it was doubt.

A lot of it was fear.

And probably a dose of fatigue and burnout mixed in.

FATIGUE AND FEAR LOVE TO WORK TOGETHER TO DERAIL US. THEY WILL OFTEN JOIN FORCES TO UNDERMINE OUR RESOLVE.

Fatigue and fear love to work together to derail us. In Peter's case, perhaps it was that growing fatigue of unmet expectations. Just a few short years ago, he had been drawn to a man who called him toward a higher purpose, something bigger and radical. But what now?

Fatigue and fear will often join forces to undermine our resolve. In Peter's case, it's possible that his growing fatigue stemmed from his *Type I* desire for things to move quicker, for change to happen, and for the things that Jesus taught to become a cultural reality. He left fishing because he believed change was coming and this Rabbi would usher it in. He was captivated by a man who beckoned him toward a higher purpose, something grand and revolutionary. But after three years, he's tired and the man he followed is dead. What now?

"What now?" also echoed in my mind as I sat in Seattle, watching the rain pour down relentlessly and recognizing that unmet expectations lay at the heart of my growing frustration. Reflecting on the decision to move, I came to the sobering realization that my move to Seattle had been a reactive step backward in an attempt to accomplish my own unfulfilled hopes and dreams. I probably blamed God a bit too.

In Las Vegas, things hadn't unfolded as I had anticipated. People didn't respond as I had hoped, the church didn't experience the rapid growth I had envisioned, and God didn't intervene in the manner I had expected. So faced with these disappointments, I retreated.

From an early age, we're fed a narrative: "Dream big dreams! Anything is within your reach!" *Type I's* are the most likely to buy into this fragile philosophy. While it's true that we should aspire to lofty goals, we must also come to terms with the reality that not everything is attainable. Frequently, our dreams materialize in ways we never foresaw. Sometimes, they unravel entirely, only for us to realize that we emerge stronger because of it. Often the dreams and aspirations we have are out of alignment with God and it is best that they NOT become a reality.

But when faced with disappointment and unmet desires, our instinctive reaction is often to retreat backward.

Three months had passed since my return to Seattle, and there I was, seated in yet another routine staff meeting. The preceding months had been consumed by the tasks of relocating my family and embedding myself in my leadership role at the church. As we made decisions and charted a course for the church's future, there were moments of undeniable synergy and impact—times when my *Type I* felt fully engaged, alive, and invigorated.

But those moments were fleeting.

I mostly felt lost, disoriented, and strangely uncomfortable.

On this particular morning, as I sat in our customary weekly leadership meeting with the pastoral team, my friend-turned-boss occupied his usual position at the head of the table. I sat in my designated spot directly opposite him, gazing across the expanse of the 12-foot-long table with our team arranged along both sides. While I can't recall the specific topic of discussion that day, I distinctly remember the moment when "IT" occurred.

You've probably witnessed that "IT" moment in movies before when the camera zooms in rapidly on two objects. In this case, it was two people. I was one of them, and my friend was the other. At that moment, everything else seemed to fade away as we sat face to face. The zoom was swift, the scene hazy, but undeniably real.

As the zoom reached its zenith, a thought engulfed my brain—a thought that had been lurking beneath the surface, suppressed but ever-present: *I. Don't. Belong. Here.*

Ok. If I'm being honest, the thought may have been more like, *What the &#% am I doing here?* But I'm committed to keeping this book PG.

I instantly felt sick, a wave of nausea washing over me. It was so intense that I had to excuse myself from the room, rising unsteadily to my feet and stumbling down the hallway. Eventually, I found refuge in a secluded, dimly lit corridor at the back of the church. I plopped myself onto the ground, curled up into a ball, my face buried in my knees, arms wrapped tightly around my legs as I began to shake uncontrollably.

After a few minutes of sitting in solitude, I reached for my phone and called my wife. "You need to come pick me up," I said firmly. "Now." Surprisingly, she didn't press for an explanation but quickly made the 30-minute drive to retrieve me.

No one else knew what had happened. They assumed I had just eaten some questionable teriyaki chicken—a common culinary experience in Seattle. But it was much bigger and deeper than that. It was my metaphorical "middle-of-the-lake" moment, a point of intense discontent where I yearned to be anywhere but where I was.

I use the term "middle-of-the-lake" because that's where Peter eventually found himself. After witnessing Jesus' death and discovering His empty tomb three days later, Peter simply retreated. Once courageous and bold, Peter, the fisher of men, reverted to his former life—a fisher of fish. He just couldn't come to terms with Jesus' death. It was beyond his comprehension, leaving him feeling bewildered, fatigued, and overwhelmed by his own failure. And when you're experiencing that flood of emotional turmoil, you instinctively retreat to seek refuge in what feels familiar.

For Peter, that was found within the confines of a fishing boat in the dead of night. For me, I sought refuge in the comfort of the familiar surroundings of the Pacific Northwest.

How had I found myself in this situation? Why had I returned to a place where I felt so out of place? Why was I exactly where I wasn't supposed to be? God had clearly called me to move from my Seattle season on to a new chapter in Las Vegas, yet in my frustration and weariness, I gave in and retreated. I had no one to blame but myself.

That Tuesday morning, at the conference table, it all came to a head and hit this *Type I* square in the face.

It's the same type of moment Peter had when a familiar voice shouted from the shore.

> *Early in the morning, Jesus stood on the shore, but the disciples did not realize that it was Jesus.*
>
> *He called out to them, "Friends, haven't you any fish?"*
>
> *"No," they answered.*
>
> *He said, "Throw your net on the right side of the boat and you will find some." When they did, they were unable to haul the net in because of the large number of fish.*
>
> *Then the disciple Jesus loved said to Peter, "It's the Master!" When Simon Peter realized that it was the Master, he threw on some clothes, for he was stripped for work, and dove into the sea. The other disciples came in by boat for they weren't far from land, a hundred yards or so, pulling along the net full of fish. When they got out of the boat, they saw a fire laid, with fish and bread cooking on it. (John 21:7-9, NIV)*

The voice resonating from the shore echoed the same call that had once beckoned him away from the life he had assumed WOULD always be his, toward a future he never COULD have imagined would be his.

Jesus was standing on the shore, His voice carrying that same compelling invitation that had captured Peter before. It was happening all over again—a deja vu of eternal proportions.

And at that moment Peter stood up in the boat.

I wonder if a cascade of memories suddenly flooded Peter's mind—every miraculous moment and profound encounter from the previous three years rushing back to him. And as those memories ebbed away, he must have found himself questioning why he was now back out on the water, in the dead of night, amidst the same familiar, but now foreign surroundings.

What was the attraction and the pull?

Why had he returned to where he no longer belonged?

THE ATTRACTION OF BACKWARD

> OUR SELECTIVE MEMORIES CAN BE PARTICULARLY
> SWEET WHEN OUR PRESENT ISN'T PRETTY.

We all do it. It's a human tendency. We put a fresh coat of paint of selective embellishment on the memories of our past and add a second coat of nostalgia to cover up the rough spots. Our selective memories can be particularly sweet when our present isn't pretty. During tough times, we often find ourselves longing for the familiarity of what's behind us. After all, why move forward when the past seems so much more appealing?

At times, we may even find ourselves romanticizing the chaos of the past—the mediocre friendships, the fleeting moments of joy in turbulent relationships, or the comfort of familiar streets in a city we were called to leave behind. This may seem contradictory to a *Type I's* nature, but we're all susceptible to these longings and tendencies. The allure of the past, with its sense of safety and familiarity, can be incredibly enticing, especially during seasons of exhaustion and disappointment, even if that feeling of safety is merely an illusion.

I want to pause here and re-acknowledge the fact that there are unique challenges to living as a *Type I*. The tendencies and wirings that make a *Type I* healthy, that enable them to contribute to their communities, create new initiatives, build strong businesses, and lead growing churches are also the tendencies that can produce parachute moments. Being the key decision-maker is tiring sometimes, regardless if the responsibility is self-inflicted. Sometimes you just want to fade into the background for a while, let the crazy world go by, and ignore that fire in your belly. But those feelings are fleeting. Our God-given wiring needs guardrails, not suppression.

Those belly-fire beliefs, seemingly unfulfilled, can also pull you backward.

OUR GOD-GIVEN WIRING NEEDS GUARDRAILS, NOT SUPPRESSION.

THE AWKWARDNESS OF BACKWARD

I still have my high school letterman jacket. I wore it with pride for the final two years of my high school tenure, even if my letter was in golf. Four straight years. I know you're jealous because what could possibly be cooler than being a member of the high school golf team? Move aside, quarterbacks!

And let's not forget the lack of fancy embroidery on the back of my jacket, a luxury my family couldn't afford. No, mine was a plain jacket, adorned only with the large letter "A" that signified my elite athletic achievement. Don't let my sarcasm fool you. To me, that letter meant everything. I wore it with pride, particularly during those significant social gatherings of 1980s high school life—Friday night football games.

For over three decades, my letterman jacket remained untouched, hanging quietly in the depths of our closet. Then a few years back, its moment to shine arrived unexpectedly. My daughter found herself in need of "throwback" attire for an 80s-themed party. I had the perfect prop. She followed me to the bedroom where I unearthed my cherished letterman jacket in all its nostalgic glory.

As she slipped it on, she was convinced she had struck gold. With her authentic, vintage 80s look, she would be the envy of her friends. However, her excitement turned to curiosity when she reached into the pockets and discovered a treasure trove of relics—a pack of Hubba Bubba chewing gum (unchewed, still in wrapper - don't be gross) and a half-used lip-gloss. The gum was mine. The lip gloss belonged to my girlfriend at the time ... who is now my wife. It was a cool moment.

They persuaded me to indulge in a bit of nostalgia and try on the jacket for old-time's sake. Reluctantly, I went for it. As I struggled, I quickly realized that it no longer fit me—not even close. In all honesty, it shouldn't have. Too many years had gone by for it to accommodate me still. The jacket was a cherished memento of bygone times, each memory sewn into its fabric. But it wasn't a place to get stuck.

Let's face it. Wearing my high school letterman's jacket as part of my weekly wardrobe wouldn't be the wisest move. It would be...well, awkward. You know, like those guys from your class who still squeeze into their high school football jerseys every Friday night and head to their alma mater stadium, trying to relive their glory days. It's a bit sad.

I think we could say it this way: *Looking back is appropriate. Going backward is awkward.*

LOOKING BACK IS APPROPRIATE. GOING BACKWARD IS AWKWARD.

Yes, we must always be aware and learn from the past. We would be foolish not to keep those memories and moments to draw from in the future, both our biggest wins and greatest losses. Those crucial snippets from our lives are part of our story and become the training ground for our ongoing development. Learning from our past and living in our past are on appropriate opposite ends of the nostalgia spectrum.

What is it about the past that keeps pulling us back? Why do we find comfort and security in places that, truth be told, never offered much of either in the first place?

Are we forgetful? Frightened? Fatigued?

When Peter encountered Christ for the second time on the shores of the Sea of Galilee, he faced a pivotal decision: either give up on following Jesus altogether or confront his failures and his fears head-on so that he could move forward.

Peter chose forward.

Literally.

Without hesitation, he leaped into the water and began swimming towards shore—an unmistakably *Type I* move if there ever was one! It may have made more sense to remain in the safety of the boat. In fact, I wouldn't be surprised if the other disciples sailed right past Peter as he embarked on his swim towards Jesus. They probably reached Jesus before him. But Peter was never one to stay calm or wait patiently. So, with characteristic impulsiveness, he dove in, swam like Michael Phelps, and arrived at the shore dripping wet, to find Jesus already preparing breakfast.

I'm a huge breakfast enthusiast. It's a non-negotiable part of my daily routine—an event that simply cannot be skipped. I'm not talking about a quick bowl of cereal or hastily prepared toast. I have my go-to breakfast spots that I frequent a few times a week, and for me, breakfast sets the tone for the rest of my day. And let's not forget the magic word: hashbrowns.

Breakfast holds a special place in my heart.

It seems that Jesus, in his divine wisdom also understood the importance of breakfast. So, if you are wondering *What Jesus Would Do?* He would eat breakfast. But in this encounter with Peter, this breakfast wasn't just a meal—it was a divine collision, an opportunity for reconnection and restoration, all with a waterfront view. Who would've thought that Jesus was also a short-order cook?

Gathered around the crackling fire, Peter and Jesus' collision transformed into a heartfelt conversation—a moment of profound invitation for Peter to make his way back. It was a call to abandon the longing for another time and place, whether filled with highs or lows and instead, wholeheartedly embrace the journey toward the person he was destined to become in this new and thrilling chapter of his life.

I can't help but wonder if this was the first time Peter sat beside a fire since that fateful night when he denied knowing Jesus. If so, how appropriate that amidst the warmth of the flames, Jesus extended a gracious invitation for Peter to reverse his trajectory—from drifting backward to forging ahead with a powerful comeback.

> *After breakfast, Jesus said to Simon Peter, "Simon, son of John, do you love me more than these?"*
>
> *"Yes, Master; you know I love you."*
>
> *Jesus said, "Feed my lambs."*
>
> *He then asked a second time, "Simon, son of John, do you love me?"*
>
> *"Yes, Master; you know I love you."*
>
> *Jesus said, "Shepherd my sheep."*
>
> *Then he said it a third time: "Simon, son of John, do you love me?"*
>
> *Peter was upset that he asked for the third time, "Do you love me?" so he answered, "Master, you know everything there is to know. You've got to know that I love you." (John 21:15-19, NIV)*

Jesus is pressing in and not holding back. He is determined to restore Peter but he's not going to make it simple and easy for him. Jesus wants Peter to recognize that his life as a fisherman is over—it's a closed chapter, not a safety net to nostalgically cling to.

It was who Peter WAS, not who Peter was NOW.

FOLLOW ME

Jesus' first invitation to Peter was simple, *"Follow me,"* (Mark 4:19, NIV). His final words to Peter? *"You MUST follow me,"* (John 21:19, NIV).

The first time Peter said yes, but faltered and reverted back. However, the second time, Peter's response was unwavering. He said yes and never looked back. This was his ultimate comeback, and this time, he fully committed to following Jesus like never before.

In the coming years, the responsibilities and leadership roles that awaited him would leave no room for halfway devotion. Jesus needed Peter to be fully invested, to be all in. And miraculously, He provided the pathway for Peter's comeback to unfold. Plus Peter got breakfast.

In my own journey, I found myself in need of that same pathway. Leaving the church office that fateful Tuesday, I found myself seated in the passenger seat of my wife's car, enveloped in a heavy silence. It was the beginning of a rapid unraveling. Emotionally, I plummeted to rock bottom. Going backward will do that to you.

It had taken its toll. I would spend long, tearful nights on the floor, wrestling with God, seeking answers to the question of what lay ahead and why this had happened. I engaged in soul-searching conversations with family and friends, as well as with the church leadership I was now serving. These conversations were difficult. They had expected one thing when they hired me, but instead, they found themselves confronted with a broken, burned-out leader.

Clarity eluded me in those moments, stranded in the middle of the lake. Everything seemed blurry and bewildering. It felt like the end of the leadership road for me. Collisions that put you face-to-face with God's desired destination have a way of doing that to you.

These types of backward-facing collision encounters leave a lasting impact, stirring our emotions and sparking inner conflict. All those elements were present. When a simple fender-bender happens, frustration is followed by an exchange of information and a quick resolution—it's irritating but manageable. When a life-altering collision happens, it disrupts the direction and lives of all involved. The intended destination is abruptly interrupted, and the path forward has to be realigned.

I thought this collision signaled the end.

It wasn't.

Jesus was still there, patiently waiting on the shore. All I had to do was recognize His voice once again, and then I had to leap into the water.

It turns out all I needed was a gentle nudge. Several months after that pivotal moment in the conference room, my wife and I found ourselves seated in the office of a life coach/therapist. We had been seeing her for a few weeks, slowly unraveling the threads of our life journey. She listened intently, asked probing questions, and together we searched for answers.

On this particular day, we were exposing the depths of our hearts, confronting the frustrations and unmet expectations that had led us to her doorstep. Out of the blue, she suddenly but softly said, "You need to go home." It caught me off guard. I remember asking, "Excuse me?" She repeated herself. We tried to explain that we didn't even know where "home" was anymore, but she insisted.

IN THE MIDST OF CHAOS, FIND THE GROUND TO BE GAINED

Two months later, we decided to pack up our brand-new home in Seattle and reset our lives in Las Vegas. I'm aware this may seem like another example of going back. However, the difference is that I chose to return to Seattle as an escape. God chose to return us to Las Vegas because He wasn't finished using us there.

Peter's comeback story began with him jumping out of a boat, and mine began with me 'jumping' into a moving truck.

Once again, I climbed into the cab of that truck with all my possessions safely tucked in the back. I headed down those same highways I had traveled just a few months earlier. Instead of excitement, this journey home was filled with fear and trepidation. I felt like I had failed twice, first by leaving Las Vegas *and* now Seattle.

But I had a gracious Savior who stood on the beach and called me back to Himself, back to the calling He had originally given me and always had for me.

Because of Jesus, it was my comeback.

For me, jumping in the water meant embarking on a long, humbling journey back. Just over one year later, I packed up that same moving truck and retraced my steps down the same freeways that had carried me to the middle of my metaphorical lake. I packed and unpacked the same boxes, which forced me to simplify my life. Life hack: If you want to streamline your belongings, try moving twice in one year—you'll quickly figure out what's essential and what's not.

One of my life axioms is this: In the midst of chaos, find the ground to be gained. The wisest people I've associated with in my life always seem to make the most out of life's most chaotic moments. While most of us are panicking, they are looking for opportunity. Opportunity to grow. Opportunity to expand. Opportunity for change and advance. Every comeback begins in chaos. However, the ability and willingness to prayerfully seek out and find that ground is the entry point of every comeback.

That's why everyone loves a great comeback story. Whether it's in sports or life, there's something inspiring about witnessing someone overcome adversity and claim victory. We were stunned when the Patriots mounted a stunning second-half comeback after being down 28-3 to win the 2017 Super Bowl. LeBron James' Cavaliers rallying from a 3-1 deficit against the Golden State Warriors to clinch the 2016 NBA title. These moments remind us that a comeback is still possible no matter how dark the situation may seem. And regardless of our allegiances, we can all appreciate and respect the power of a great comeback.

If you've experienced failure or found yourself living life in the rearview mirror, you're actually in a prime position for a comeback.

Jesus restored an unfaithful Peter.

He chose a tax collector to be his disciple.

He used a scandalized woman to start a revival.

He called Judas "friend."

He promised paradise to a thief.

How could He not be for you?

Peter stumbled and failed, yet Jesus chose him to lead His worldwide revolution. Who does that? Jesus does. That's the power of Jesus' grace. Peter's failure became his pathway forward. And because Peter was willing enough to jump out of a boat, Jesus initiated a comeback.

As a *Type I*, you may feel like you haven't met God's expectations – maybe you haven't even met your *own* expectations – or if you've messed up or embarrassed yourself or gone back to a life you left behind – you are now perfectly situated to be a recipient of God's grace. It's time to find the ground to be gained. Look around. It may be your middle-of-the-lake moment where the next move you need to make involves a leap out of the boat and into the raging waters of what's next.

So dive in.

You have permission.

JESUS RESTORED AN UNFAITHFUL PETER.
HE CHOSE A TAX COLLECTOR TO BE HIS DISCIPLE.
HE USED A SCANDALIZED WOMAN TO START A REVIVAL.
HE CALLED JUDAS "FRIEND."
HE PROMISED PARADISE TO A THIEF.
HOW COULD HE NOT BE FOR YOU?

KEY TAKEAWAYS AND DISCUSSION STARTERS:

1. THE TEMPTATION TO RETREAT: When faced with challenges and uncertainties, people often feel tempted to retreat to what feels familiar and comfortable, even if it means going back to a previous stage in life. However, this backward movement rarely leads to a positive outcome. It's important to recognize when the desire to retreat is driven by fear, fatigue, or unmet expectations.

- What is a way that you keep yourself from retreating into comfortability?
- Talk about a time when you chose to press forward through something uncomfortable.

2. RECOGNIZING DISPLACEMENT: There are moments in life when we suddenly realize that we don't belong where we are. This feeling of displacement can be overwhelming and lead to questioning our choices and circumstances. Whether it's a sudden realization or a gradual understanding, acknowledging that we are in the wrong place is the first step toward change.

- Do you have a plan for self-evaluation? How would you know if you are in the wrong place?

3. THE POWER OF COMEBACK: Despite failures, mistakes, and moments of doubt, it's possible to experience a comeback. Just as Peter experienced restoration and a renewed sense of purpose after his moment of denial, individuals can also find redemption and direction by embracing their failures and moving forward with courage and faith. A comeback is not about erasing past mistakes but learning from them and allowing them to propel us toward a better future.

- What do you think of when you hear the term, "comeback?"
- Who do you know who might need a renewed sense of purpose?

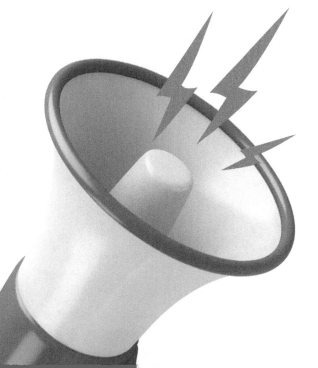

CHAPTER 10

CONCLUSION

．．．．．．．．．．．

So our journey now takes us full circle, from the shores of the Sea of Galilee to the shores of Lake Washington. When our family was living in Seattle, we decided to take a day excursion to the University of Washington Shell house. We rented two canoes with all the accessories. My wife and daughter loaded into one while my son Austin and I carefully stepped into the other. With life jackets securely in place and oars in hand, we headed confidently out into the waters of Lake Washington.

We've all had experiences where the idea was way more ideal than the actual execution. My wife and I had a glorious image of what a day on the water would be like, and the memories we would make with our kids. We even packed a picnic lunch. However, my idealism quickly shifted to insanity as my son and I attempted to navigate the choppy waters brought on by the wake of the other boats. Within a short time, we were completely trapped on the lake, rowing vigorously (well, as vigorously as an 8-year-old can row) and making zero progress. At one point, Austin began to panic and this manifested itself with loud screaming alongside accusations that I was failing him as a father.

He wasn't completely wrong.

By virtue of a miracle, we eventually returned to the dock, where we were informed that most of our issues were caused by sitting in the wrong positions in the canoe. Our positioning was off. The small guy (Austin) should have been in the back and I should have held down the bow position. Because of this mistake, our weight distribution was off making it nearly impossible to steer the boat. We never got in full sync which caused us to basically be fighting each other even as we rowed more feverishly. All of that combined with our general ineptitude was a recipe for disaster. Our ideal afternoon quickly became a nightmare. Oh, my wife and daughter were just fine. They cruised around the waters like there was no resistance. They were smiling and laughing. But Austin and I? We were frustrated and miserable. So much so, that we didn't even want to stay and enjoy our family picnic. We chewed our sandwiches, put on a fake smile, and then rode home in silence.

That exact location in a different era yielded a completely different picture. It's a dreary, drizzly cold morning, in the fall of 1935 as nine men make their way across Lake Washington, rowing vigorously both for speed and to keep their hands from freezing. Why are they out there on a day when no one should be braving these elements? Their objective is the hope of progress. They are the rowing team from the University of Washington in the aptly named Husky Clipper. While the rest of the city shelters, this crew leans into the opportunity to incrementally hone their harmony just a bit more.

Although they rowed in obscurity this particular morning, their sport, Crew, was anything but unknown. Rowing is not a sport most of us are currently aware of or follow. Perhaps we caught a glimpse as we flipped through the channels during the summer Olympics. However, this was not the case in the early 1900s. Elite colleges from the East Coast fielded superior teams typically dominating the sport, while a few small schools from California and Washington slowly rose to dominate the West Coast. Assembled from various life narratives and motivations, this diverse nine-man crew shared the same desired destination. And it took hundreds of these uncomfortable, early mornings on the lake to make their dream a reality.

This team's challenges and accomplishments are recounted in the fabulous book *Boys in the Boat* by Daniel James Brown. These young men came together from various backgrounds, embraced and submitted to the leadership around them, and eventually experienced their greatest triumph, a gold medal in the 1936 Olympic games.

Because the sport is often overlooked, it's easy to miss the dynamics and lessons tucked beneath its surface, as the team glides swiftly across the water. When we look closely, we will see the makings of a fast, successful rowing team and the blueprint for an impactful organizational team. This story is more than just a typical Depression-era sports underdog story, the narrative of these boys in the boat offers profound insights into the art of assembling a winning team from diverse parts and underscores the importance of teamwork, trust, and leadership.

SEARCHING FOR "SWING"

First the basics.

An eight-man crew is actually a team of nine. Picture this: eight rowers working to propel the shell (or boat) through the water in perfect synchrony while the coxswain sits at the helm, facing the crew, loudly leading them toward the finish line. Rowing competitions are varied, ranging from lightning-fast sprints covering a distance of 2000 meters to grueling endurance tests spanning a demanding 4-mile course. Regardless of the distance, each race commences with a flurry of activity as the flag drops or the sound of the starting gun echoes across the water and the tactical sprint ensues.

In that exhilarating moment, strategy and skill converge as the crew burst into action, their rhythmic strokes propelling them forward with precision and power. It's something—the fluid motion of oars slicing through the water, the determined expressions on each rower's face, and the steady guidance provided by the coxswain. (*Note: this is NOT how Austin and I looked as we thrashed about on that beautiful Saturday afternoon.*)

Every team member plays a vital role as the race unfolds, from the rowers' sheer strength and endurance to the coxswain's tactical expertise. Together, they navigate the twists and turns of the course, responding to the ebb and flow of the competition. Rowing is more than just a sport—it's a picture of the power of teamwork, dedication, and resilience. As the crew pushes themselves to the limit, each stroke brings them closer to the finish line and the satisfaction of a well-rowed race.

Additionally, rowing operates on a different principle. Unlike other team sports where a single superstar like Jordan, Ohtani, or Messi can often carry an entire team to victory through their individual efforts and skill, success on the water hinges not on the prowess of one exceptional athlete, but on the collective harmony of the entire team. The entire shell suffers if one person in the boat is out of sync. It's as if a heavy weight drags down each stroke, slowing the progress of the entire crew. But when everyone pulls together, the shell seems to glide effortlessly through the water, as if propelled by an invisible force.

What's remarkable is that within any rowing crew, you'll find a diverse mix of personalities, strengths, and skills. Each individual brings something unique to the table, contributing to the overall efficiency and competency of the team. From the powerhouse rowers driving the boat forward to the strategic guidance of the coxswain, every member plays a crucial role in the team's success.

> NO MATTER HOW TALENTED OR SKILLED WE MAY BE AS INDIVIDUALS, OUR GREATEST ACHIEVEMENTS ARE OFTEN REALIZED WHEN WE WORK TOGETHER AS A UNIFIED TEAM.

In essence, rowing teaches us a valuable lesson: no matter how talented or skilled we may be as individuals, our greatest achievements are often realized when we work together as a unified team. This collective effort, this shared commitment to excellence, propels us to victory, stroke by stroke, decision by decision, action by action.

In rowing, this is known as *swing*. This is not a simple accomplishment, hence the hours of early mornings out on the water. *"Many crews, even winning crews, never really find it,"* writes

Brown. "It only happens when all eight oarsmen are rowing in such perfect unison that no single action by anyone is out of sync with those of all the others…Only then will the boat continue to run, unchecked, fluidly and gracefully, between pulls of the oars. Only then will it feel as if the boat is a part of each of them, moving as if on its own."[1]

> TO BE IN SYNC, EACH INDIVIDUAL MUST RECOGNIZE AND APPRECIATE THEIR TEAMMATES UNIQUE CONTRIBUTIONS WHILE CONFIDENTLY EMBRACING THEIR SPECIFIC ROLE TO PROPEL THE TEAM FORWARD.

Finding that elusive rhythm isn't merely about rowing as hard as humanly possible and exerting maximum effort—it's about rowing in perfect harmony. To synchronize with others, each individual must recognize and appreciate the unique contributions of their teammates while confidently fulfilling their own specific role in propelling the team forward. This fundamental principle holds significant meaning when considering the intense complexities of effective leadership in any organization or endeavor. Within this team pursuit of swing lies a pivotal role that can either make or break the journey.

AS IN CREW, SO AS IN LIFE

Undoubtedly, the coxswain is the ultimate leadership figure within the rowing team, carrying a multitude of responsibilities essential for the team's success. The coxswain's role is indispensable from steering the boat to ensuring communication among crew members, providing motivation, and determining strategic maneuvers during races.

Affectionately known as the "Cox" within rowing circles, this individual assumes the central role in determining the crew's fate. Positioned in the bow, their face adorned with a strange yet functional megaphone resembling a tilted party hat, the coxswain becomes the voice of guidance and encouragement as the race intensifies. Through this megaphone, they relay vital instructions, maintain morale with timely words of encouragement, and regulate the pace for the rowers stretched out along the 80-foot expanse of the shell.

In essence, the coxswain embodies a large and loud presence, responsible for maintaining harmony among the eight rowers. What's fascinating is physically, the coxswain is rarely the most athletic member of the crew. Smaller in stature, but large and loud in leadership, the coxswain is both coach and strategist, serving as the mastermind behind the rowers' physical prowess. They juggle multiple roles—navigator, strategist, analyst, communicator, motivator, coach, and commander—each vital to the team's success.

The complexity of the coxswain's role sets them apart from the rowers they guide. While the rowers excel in physical strength, the coxswain's leadership, vision, and strategic acumen drive the team forward. Their ability to synthesize information, make split-second decisions, and inspire their crewmates is pivotal in the fast-paced world of competitive rowing. *"From the moment the shell is launched, the coxswain is the captain,"* wrote Daniel James Brown." *"He or she must exert control, both physical and psychological, over everything that goes on in the shell."*[2]

As in crew, so in life. The leaders of the boat – or a business or country – set the tone for everyone else and often determine whether that enterprise will be successful. This holds true for any group endeavor, from a rowing team to a teammate, to a business, to a church. To get in "the swing" and make real progress together, leaders, especially *Type I* leaders, must create an atmosphere of trust, clarity, collaboration, and belonging that filters down to everyone involved.

TO GET IN "THE SWING," LEADERS MUST CREATE AN ATMOSPHERE OF TRUST, CLARITY, COLLABORATION, AND BELONGING THAT FILTERS DOWN TO EVERYONE INVOLVED.

This is a picture of the challenges of moving an organization toward a desired goal, including the alignment, management, and motivation needed to keep everyone and everything moving in the same direction. That was Peter's new reality as the early Christ followers became the early church. Peter's transformation from Simon to Peter was now complete. The journey and learnings of the past led to the fulfillment of Peter's calling. Perhaps that is where you find yourself too. You are at the point that requires the *Type I* in you to step up and stand up.

Again, Brown captures this idea so well, *"Good crews are good blends of personalities: someone to lead the charge, someone to hold something in reserve; someone to pick a fight, someone to make peace; someone to think things through, someone to charge ahead without thinking."*[3]

As we move into the book of Acts, the narrative history of the early days of the church, and what would become a global movement of faith, I couldn't get this image out of my mind. I see Peter. He's attempting to do his best to assemble a rag-tag group of early followers who have been swimming in uncertainty and chaos since Jesus' arrest and crucifixion. They went from devastation to elation.

When Jesus appears at that moment to encourage and mobilize them, they're given the ultimate assignment (see Matthew 28) to carry the gospel to the ends of the earth. That's a huge mission, one that comes with some overarching instructions and the assurance that he will return. Then he's gone. This gap demanded and pointed to the desperate need for a strong *Type I*, someone who will bravely and courageously stand up to lead.

In this moment, I see Peter's determination to ignite hope in his companions. Despite their despair, he fires up their faith with his unwavering belief in Jesus' victory over death. It's a pivotal moment—a turning point that sets the stage for the remarkable journey ahead. In it, I'm reminded of the transformative power of faith to triumph over darkness and lead to boundless opportunities.

There are two initial moments that scream *Type I* leadership, which indicate Peter is ready to lead, has been forged to lead and is finally humble enough to lead. In many ways, Peter will be at a crossroads where he will be invited (perhaps forced) to lead. The high-capacity leadership that Jesus saw deep in Peter will now need to come to the surface. His leadership or lack thereof would set the tone. His *Type I* would be both needed and stretched. These initial moments would define Peter's leadership of this world-altering movement...or lack thereof.

The pictures we have of these crucial early moments are provided by Luke, the writer of Acts, as he records the early history of the church. First, as the disciples, now the leaders of this movement, consider what's next in the absence of Judas, we read, *"In those days Peter **stood up** among the believers, a group numbering about a hundred and twenty" (Acts 1:15, NIV).* Like a coxswain, Peter assumes leadership, offering clear direction and providing precisely what is needed.

He stood up.

It shouldn't surprise us that in the midst of questioning what's next, it's no wonder that Peter, embodying the traits of a *Type I* individual, stood up and rose to the occasion. He embraced and fully exercised his *Type I*, which required a full transition from his former identity as Simon to now completely embody the confidence of Peter. Decisions were looming, leadership was vital, and all eyes naturally turned to Peter. With characteristic boldness, Peter stepped into the role, drawing upon his wealth of experiences and learning from past failures.

Then, just a few days later, Peter again took center stage as the Holy Spirit's presence swept through the room where they had gathered, capturing the attention of the entire city of Jerusalem. *"Then Peter **stood up** with the Eleven, raised his voice, and addressed the crowd: "Fellow Jews and all of you who live in Jerusalem, let me explain this to you; listen carefully to what I say." (Acts 2:14, NIV).* The moment demanded a spokesperson. It demanded courage. It demanded boldness.

Peter exhibits remarkable boldness in proclaiming Jesus' message, even in the face of opposition and persecution. On that day, he delivered a powerful sermon, fearlessly declaring the gospel to a crowd of thousands. Despite the potential risks, Peter does not shy away from boldly sharing his faith.

These early moments illuminate Peter's realization: when Jesus said his final words, giving this massive and ultimate mission to "go into the entire world and make followers," this wasn't just a suggestion but a call to action that would require every aspect of his *Type I* to accomplish this enormous mission. The mission became the destination: go into the entire world. And every bit of Peter's leadership would be tested as he embarked on this massive endeavor.

THE PRIORITY OF CONFIDENCE AND CLARITY

TYPE I INDIVIDUALS ARE TYPICALLY HIGHLY MOTIVATED, BUT THEY EXCEL WHEN THEY ARE PROVIDING CLARITY AND CONFIDENCE TO OTHERS.

For any of this to be possible, Peter would have to quickly learn how to mobilize, align, and empower those who stood eagerly alongside in this journey. *Type I* individuals are typically highly motivated, but they operate best when they are providing clarity and confidence to others. It's reflected in what Jack Nicholson famously said in the classic film, *A Few Good Men*, *"You want me on that wall. You need me on that wall."* This sentiment rings true of *Type I's*. Are we sometimes irritating? Absolutely. Intense? No doubt. But it's precisely these qualities that enable us to boldly venture into unknown and uncharted territories. When we're willing to navigate the intricacies of a *Type I* individual, we unlock endless opportunities and unleash their full potential.

And in the midst of Peter standing up, we see a *Type I* leader taking the helm at the front of the boat. This seasoned fisherman, accustomed to a life spent on the water, now assumes the pivotal role of the early church's coxswain, guiding and directing those tasked with spreading the Good News to every corner of the earth. He begins to chart their course. He motivates, propelling them forward. He directs, pointing them constantly towards the destination. He breaks new ground, a pivotal moment in the expansion of the early church.

While this assignment may seem tailor-made for a *Type I* individual—appearing to be simple, straightforward, and seamless—we have to recognize the hour-by-hour, day-to-day challenges of assigning tasks, mobilizing resources, and keeping the group in alignment with accomplishing their mission.

The journey from the shores of the Sea of Galilee to the heart of the stormy sea, from boldly stepping out onto the water to standing atop the Mount of Transfiguration to even enduring his darkest hours in a courtyard during Jesus' trial—all of these experiences accumulated, empowering Peter to walk confidently in the identity that Jesus had given him. Now, he is stepping forward to lead with assurance and conviction.

Now, all those early followers of Jesus found themselves walking alongside Peter, a transformed, different type of leader—a *Type I*. His initiative, intensity, and innovation were not diminished but heightened, becoming even more crucial for the movement's forward momentum.

Throughout this early period of the church, Peter would continually confront issues and challenges head-on. He courageously called out Ananias and Sapphira for their lies regarding their giving, resulting in their deaths, and emphasized the importance of genuine generosity within the community. He listened attentively to God's guidance, which led him to the house of Cornelius, where he learned that Gentiles were to be welcomed into the kingdom of God. It's clear that Peter was the perfect candidate for innovation and disruption within the early church because of his *Type I* - not despite it.

As we reflect on Peter's journey and transformation into a dynamic leader within the early Christian community, let's ponder how we can embody these qualities. Let's strive to emulate Peter's growth and embrace traits such as humility, gentleness, patience, and love—qualities that may not have been immediately apparent in his earlier years but undoubtedly became markers of his leadership as he matured in his faith.

Peter's words, most likely penned near the end of his life, offer valuable insights for *Type I* leaders. He talks about traits that may not have been initially associated with him but now can be used to describe those of us who reflect this leadership style.

So don't lose a minute in building on what you've been given, complementing your basic faith with good character, spiritual understanding, alert discipline, passionate patience, reverent wonder, warm friendliness, and generous love, each dimension fitting into and developing the others. With these qualities active and growing in your lives, no grass will grow under your feet, no day will pass without its reward as you mature in your experience of our Master Jesus. (2 Peter 1 5-9, MSG)

IF YOU'RE A HIGH-CAPACITY, TYPE I LEADER, WE'RE COUNTING ON YOU — YOUR DRIVE, YOUR INNOVATION, YOUR INTENSITY — ARE EXACTLY WHAT WE NEED TO MOVE FORWARD. AND IF YOU'RE WALKING ALONGSIDE A HIGH-CAPACITY, TYPE I LEADER, YOUR SUPPORT IS CRUCIAL.

Listen up. If you're a high-capacity, *Type I* leader, we're counting on you. Your drive, your innovation, your intensity—are exactly what we need to move forward. And if you're walking alongside a high-capacity, *Type I* leader, your support is crucial. Let them fully embrace the gifts God has given them.

If you're married to, friends with, or working alongside a high-capacity *Type I* individual, I'm praying for you. There may be moments when they drive you crazy, but I'm also praying that you'll give them the permission and space to be exactly who God created them to be. The kingdom needs them. We need them.

A healthy *Type I* leader, like Peter in Acts, embodies all the traits that make them effective and indispensable. And that health begins with leading and living in harmony—think of it as finding your SWING—with God and others.

IN SWING WITH GOD

As we close this conversation, let me encourage the *Type I's* that harmonizing your wiring and your faith requires an intentional effort to not run out from under God's desire for you. All of the shadow traits that we have discussed (conceit, control, etc.) will want to hijack the advantageous and helpful parts (innovation, inspiration, etc.) of what you bring to the table or should I say "to the boat."

In the whirlwind of activity, it's crucial to maintain a deep sense of spiritual connection and harmony with God. Instead of allowing the relentless pursuit of success to overshadow your faith, *Type I* Christians must continually cultivate an ongoing mindset of surrender and trust in God's guidance.

By relinquishing control and embracing humility, we open ourselves to divine intervention and guidance in all our endeavors. To encourage this, we must be committed to incorporating moments of stillness and reflection into our hectic schedules, which allows us to tune our hearts to the whispers and promptings of the Divine, finding solace and strength in those moments. In essence, for *Type I* Christians to stay in step and harmony with God, it's not merely about practical actions, but about fostering an awareness of His presence and guidance amidst the hustle and bustle of *Type I* living.

IN SWING WITH OTHERS

Type I 's, known for their assertiveness, ambition, and relentless pursuit of goals, often face challenges in maintaining harmony with others due to their strong-willed nature. Our innate drive to achieve can sometimes overshadow the importance of fostering cooperative and empathetic relationships. However, by recognizing the significance of empathy and understanding in interpersonal dynamics, *Type I* individuals can navigate these challenges more effectively. Instead of solely focusing on our own objectives, we can actively listen to others' perspectives, seeking to understand differing viewpoints and experiences. This empathetic approach fosters mutual respect and creates a foundation for collaboration, allowing *Type I's* to leverage the strengths of diverse team members towards shared goals.

Moreover, *Type I* individuals can cultivate patience and flexibility in their interactions to build greater harmony with others. Rather than always taking charge, look for the opportunity to empower team members by delegating tasks and trusting our abilities. This not only relieves some of the pressure *Type I's* often place on themselves but also cultivates a more inclusive and balanced team dynamic.

Additionally, embracing the art of compromise and negotiation enables *Type I's* to find common ground and resolve conflicts constructively, cultivating stronger and more harmonious relationships in both personal and professional spheres. By integrating these practices and disciplines into our relational interactions, *Type I's* can leverage their drive and determination to not only achieve individual success but also create collaborative environments where everyone can thrive.

AS A TYPE I PERSON, PRIORITIZING RELATIONAL SKILLS MIGHT NOT COME NATURALLY OR FEEL PARTICULARLY APPEALING. DO IT ANYWAY.

Caution: As a *Type I* person, prioritizing relational skills might not come naturally or feel particularly appealing. Do it anyway. Push past this inclination. When a *Type I* acknowledges the potential pitfalls of relational disconnects and takes proactive steps toward fostering harmony, it benefits everyone involved. Everyone wins.

Resisting the temptation to bulldoze through challenging relational situations and conversations is key. While it might seem like a quick fix, it ultimately damages credibility, causes people to suffer, and squanders potential opportunities.

Reflecting on the UW crew, Brown emphasized, *"What mattered more than how hard a man rowed was how well everything he did in the boat harmonized with what the other fellows were doing. And a man couldn't harmonize with his crewmates unless he opened his heart to them. He had to care about his crew."*[4]

This sentiment holds true not only in rowing but also in broader life contexts. Individual effort alone is not enough; genuine care and connection are vital for effective teamwork and collaboration.

Type I's … you have a crew. Recognize that you have a team around you—whether it's family, friends, colleagues, or clients. It's essential to genuinely care for and support these individuals, not solely to advance personal agendas but for the collective well-being and success of the team.

IN SWING WITH THE TYPES I'S YOU ARE SURROUNDED BY

Some last words to those who have read this far and learned some things about themselves, but more importantly, have a better understanding of the *Type I's* in their domain. Here's what I want to encourage you to avoid and encourage you to affirm. First, please avoid throwing their wiring back in the face of your favorite *Type I*. For example, I was recently with a church team whose leader was definitely a strong *Type I*. In the midst of our conversations, one of the team leads offered perspective on working with this senior leader. What he said was VERY revealing and also damaging. He said, "I feel like my role here is to keep on top of Matt and pull him back regularly." I remember pausing at that moment, a bit stunned and had the group take a break. The follow-up conversations were interesting, but suffice it to say, that is NOT the approach that should be taken.

Yes, guardrails for a *Type I* are significant and very important. However, an approach that seeks to dial back the healthy, needed aspects of a *Type I's* contribution is stifling, both to the individual and the organization. If you are doing life next to a *Type I*, a heavy cocktail of affirmation, acknowledgment, and assertiveness is encouraged.

AFFIRMATION: *Type I* individuals often grapple with their inherent wiring, as discussed in the Clarity chapter. An environment that is unwelcoming or fails to embrace their unique contributions can prove detrimental. Your ability to regularly encourage the *Type I* person's healthy traits to be fully exercised will be freeing.

ACKNOWLEDGMENT: Though your wiring may differ, your regular acknowledgment of *Type I* contributions is vital. Lean into those *Type I's* around you. Pour gasoline on their ingrained creativity and tenacity. Pull them into conversations, projects, and activities that feed their *Type I* souls.

ASSERTIVENESS: Surprising as it may seem, individuals with *Type I* tendencies benefit from a healthy dose of assertiveness. When situations demand it, it's crucial to be intense and firm with them. Again… a confession. Despite our intense nature, we value those who match our energy, particularly when it comes from someone who doesn't reflect a normal *Type I* response. It's essential not to shy away from directly addressing unhealthy behavior or inappropriate leadership. Do it. Keep it healthy, respectful, and as kind as possible. But do it. While we may not initially welcome the candor, it ultimately fosters credibility in our relationships and builds a foundation of trust and respect. Instead of giving in to the temptation to avoid conflict, embrace the challenge that *Type I* individuals bring to your life, which is both rewarding and frustrating.

PETER DIDN'T REJECT HIS WIRING BUT LEARNED TO SUBMIT IT FULLY TO THE TRANSFORMATION JESUS PROVIDED.

SUBMITTING YOUR TYPE I

Peter's time with Jesus provided the transformation - the refining, molding, and purifying - of his *Type I* traits for him to have permission to fully lead forward in ways he never would have been able to otherwise. He had a soul transformation. But his God-given *Type I* was still very present. He didn't reject his wiring but learned to submit it fully to the transformation Jesus provided. Jesus gently helped Peter learn how his specific traits could be leveraged in a healthy way to advance the kingdom of God. How do I wash others' feet? How do I go the extra mile? How do I turn the other cheek?

And as Peter went through his own "dark night of the soul," he made a comeback, emerging with his calling secure and in place. His assignment was then to spend the next thirty to forty years launching and leading the movement that we're still experiencing today called the Church.

Yes, there would be occasional aggressiveness and overstepping, yet Peter's leadership style effectively inspires and influences others. His passionate preaching and bold actions motivate fellow early believers to join him in the mission of spreading the gospel. Peter's leadership is marked by a sense of urgency and purpose, rallying others to actively participate in the growth of the early church.

Just as Peter had to constantly learn to align his *Type I* to confront questions and situations, we also need to learn these lessons. How do I use my *Type I* to give others courage? How do I yield it to humbly serve the Church so that the kingdom can move forward, not for my own agenda, but to see God's kingdom come? How do I mobilize my *Type I* to break through barriers and make space for others? How do I leverage it to confront injustice?

Throughout the three years that he walked with Jesus, Peter had to navigate and harness his *Type I* tendencies. Similarly, no matter where we find ourselves—whether in church leadership, the corporate world, as students, and so on—we too must learn to yield to Jesus' transformative power. This allows Him to shape and refine the *Type I* within us, enabling us to advance the mission of the church and the kingdom of God effectively.

This journey isn't about conforming to fit into a more contemplative mold by shaving off our rough edges. Instead, it's about surrendering to God's transformative work, allowing Him to mold us into the clearest picture of who He designed us to be. Through this process, His desires are fully and completely accomplished through us.

You are not just wanted; you are needed. Your family, your community, your church—they all need you. But most importantly, God invites you.

So go ahead.

Go Lead.

Go Give.

Go Serve.

Go Be Peter.

You have permission.

The world is waiting.

KEY TAKEAWAYS AND DISCUSSION STARTERS:

. . . .

EFFECTIVE LEADERSHIP DEMANDS COLLABORATION: Good leadership requires working together. A *Type I* leader leads by example, encouraging resilience, guidance, and teamwork. They guide the team while also empowering each member to contribute. Collaboration helps tap into everyone's strengths, leading to better solutions and increased productivity. It also builds trust and unity among team members, making the workplace more cohesive. So, effective leadership isn't just about one person; it's about everyone working together towards success.

- Think of the canoeing story. Have you ever realized, after the fact, that something you had worked really hard at would have been easier if you took a step back and gave yourself time to consider another way? Do you find that the situation would have been easier with a guide available to you? Why or why not?

- How do you feel you are received when you choose to offer guidance in a team-like environment?

TRANSFORMATION AND GROWTH IN LEADERSHIP: Peter has undergone profound transformation in both his personal and spiritual journey. Through his experiences and challenges, he has delved deep into his soul, emerging with newfound strength and purpose. This inner growth has empowered him to undertake extraordinary endeavors in expanding the Kingdom. With a renewed sense of faith and determination post - comeback, Peter is now capable of achieving remarkable feats, making meaningful contributions to the greater good. His journey is an example of the power of personal growth and the impact of spiritual depth.

- Do you feel equipped and empowered to be bold and take action as you grow where God has you?

- What are some steps that you might take to give yourself more opportunities to lead from your wiring?

LIVING IN HARMONY: Integrating spiritual connection and humility with assertiveness and ambition allows *Type I* individuals to align their actions with God's guidance and create collaborative environments where everyone can thrive. This integration enables them to lead with a sense of purpose and clarity, grounded in humility, but guided by divine wisdom. Their assertiveness and ambition are then tempered by a deep understanding of their role within the greater scheme of things, allowing them to lead with a leaning toward compassion and empathy. In these collaborative environments, everyone is empowered to contribute their unique talents and perspectives, resulting in group success and contentment.

- Sometimes, it's easier just to do the job yourself. How can you learn to surrender the things you hold onto so tightly to foster harmony and collaboration with the people around you?
- How do you plan on growing in your submission to God so that you can live in harmony with Him and abide in His presence?

ENDNOTES

CHAPTER 1 - CALLING: SHALLOW WATERS

1. "Calling Definition & Meaning." *Merriam-Webster*, https://www.merriam-webster.com/dictionary/calling. Accessed 8 April 2024.
2. "Calling Definition & Meaning." *Merriam-Webster*, 28 April 2024, https://www.merriam-webster.com/dictionary/calling. Accessed 2 May 2024.
3. Buechner, Frederick. *Wishful thinking*. Harper & Row, 1973.

CHAPTER 2: DEEP WATERS

1. Tozer, A.W. *The Pursuit of God*. Published January 1, 1982 by Christian Publications. ISBN 9780875093666 (ISBN10: 0875093663)
2. "Let Your Life Speak: Listening for the Voice of Vocation" (San Francisco: Jossey-Bass, 2000), p. 4

CHAPTER 3: CLARITY

1. http://www.livingwellmag.com/whats-name/#:~:text=Jesus%20addresses%20Peter%20by%20the,gives%20him%20a%20new%20name.
2. "2024 Identity Theft Facts and Statistics." *IdentityTheft.org*, https://identitytheft.org/statistics/. Accessed 2 May 2024.

CHAPTER 4: CHARACTER

1. "'Titanic' director James Cameron blames submersible's carbon-fiber hull for deadly implosion." *New York Post*, 23 June 2023, https://nypost.com/2023/06/23/james-cameron-blames-titanic-subs-carbon-fiber-hull-for-implosion/. Accessed 2 May 2024.

2. Palmer, Parker. (2017, January 29), Life on the Mobius Strip. YouTube. https://youtu.be/Qo00-zidiTQ?si=BO9D_sSLxzb5gveO

3. Sorge, Bob. *Secrets of the Secret Place Legacy Edition*. Oasis House, 2020.

CHAPTER 5: COURAGE

1. Lean In: Women, Work, and the Will to Lead, by Sheryl Sandberg. Copyright 2013 by LI Org, LLC.

CHAPTER 6: CONTROL

1. Langer, E. J. (1975). The illusion of control. Journal of Personality and Social Psychology, 32(2), 311-328.

2. Lee, J. D. (2018). It's All Under Control: A Journey of Letting Go, Hanging On, and Finding a Peace You Almost Forgot Was Possible. WaterBrook.

3. Nouwen, H. J. M. (1985). The Dance of Life: Weaving Sorrows and Blessings into One Joyful Step. Ave Maria Press.

4. Lewis, C. S. (1942). The Screwtape Letters. HarperCollins. p.27-30.

CHAPTER 7: CONCEITED

1. Didion, Joan. The Year of Magical Thinking. Knopf Doubleday Publishing Group, 2007.

2. Brooks, Arthur C. *From Strength to Strength: Finding Success, Happiness and Deep Purpose in the Second Half of Life*. Green Tree Publications, 2023.

3. Brooks, Arthur C. *From Strength to Strength: Finding Success, Happiness and Deep Purpose in the Second Half of Life*. Green

Tree Publications, 2023.

4. Barton, Ruth Haley. *Strengthening the Soul of Your Leadership: Seeking God in the Crucible of Ministry*. InterVarsity Press, 2018.

5. Witt, Lance. (2024, March 5), The Surprising Strategy for a Life of Influence. Seminar. The Crossing Church.

6. Chole, Alicia. *40 Days of Decrease: A Different Kind of Hunger. A Different Kind of Fast*. Nashville, Thomas Nelson, 2021. 14.

7. Peterson, Eugene H. "Transparent lives." *The Christian Century*, 29 November 2003, https://www.christiancentury. org/article/2003-11/transparent-lives. Accessed 2 May 2024.

8. Grant, Adam. (2024, April 2. *[Narcissistic leaders are threatened by talent. They want to be the smartest person in the room. Humble leaders are drawn to talent. They surround themselves with people who make them smarter.]. Twitter. https://twitter.com/AdamMGrant/ status/1774836192220942668.*

9. Cardinal, Rafael. "Litany of Humility." *EWTN*, https://www. ewtn.com/catholicism/devotions/litany-of-humility-245. Accessed 2 May 2024.

CHAPTER 8: COWARDICE

1. 2016, April 25). *Real World Parallels to Last Night's Episode of Silicon Valley*. Joe Lonsdale. Retrieved March 17, 2024, from http://mail.joelonsdale.com/news/real-world-parallels-last-nights-episode-silicon-valley/

2. 1947 *War As I Knew It* (1947), as cited in Oxford Dictionary of American Quotations, By Hugh Rawson, Margaret Miner, p. 258

3. "Forge Definition & Meaning." *Merriam-Webster*, 26 April 2024, https://www.merriam-webster.com/dictionary/forge. Accessed 2 May 2024.

CHAPTER 9: COMEBACK

N/A

CHAPTER 10: CONCLUSION

1. Brown, Daniel James. *The Boys in the Boat: Nine Americans and Their Epic Quest for Gold at the 1936 Berlin Olympics*. Penguin Publishing Group, 2013. p. 233.
2. Brown, Daniel James. *The Boys in the Boat: Nine Americans and Their Epic Quest for Gold at the 1936 Berlin Olympics*. Penguin Publishing Group, 2013. p. 158.
3. Brown, Daniel James. *The Boys in the Boat: Nine Americans and Their Epic Quest for Gold at the 1936 Berlin Olympics*. Penguin Publishing Group, 2013. p. 98.
4. Brown, Daniel James. *The Boys in the Boat: Nine Americans and Their Epic Quest for Gold at the 1936 Berlin Olympics*. Penguin Publishing Group, 2013. p. 134.

ABOUT THE AUTHOR

Lee brings over 30 years of experience in ministry and leadership within the local church. This experience has given him a wide understanding of churches and effective strategies, alongside his practical work serving as Executive Pastor at The Crossing Church in Las Vegas for the past 16 years.

Lee's commitment to partnering and consulting with churches across the nation is evident in his role as the president of Growmentum Group. This perspective allows him to guide churches as they align with the unique vision that God has for their community. His experience in church leadership also includes a season of student ministry and eight years of planting and pastoring in Las Vegas.

Lee has a Master's in Global Leadership from Fuller Seminary. He and his wife, Tanya, have been married for over 30 years, have lived in Vegas for the majority of that time and have two adult children. When Lee isn't speaking, coaching, or consulting, he enjoys running his favorite trails, playing golf, eating a great meal, and watching Vegas Golden Knights hockey.

CONNECT WITH LEE

Stay connected with Lee - where he's speaking,
his writing, latest leadership thoughts, and MORE!

⊕ : leecoate.com   ⊙ : @leecoate

. . . .

ABOUT ⅍ growmentum·

As a leader, being in the day-to-day work can take most of your time – leaving little for anything else. This daily work is essential, but it's equally important to regularly zoom out and gain perspective in order to work more effectively and strategically. The 'work on it' approach allows leaders to prioritize improving the organization, ultimately resulting in more efficient and productive 'work in it' days.

At Growmentum, we help you change that reality by partnering with you to work on it for greater impact – while helping you create a strategic path forward.

⊕ : growmentumgroup.com   ⊙ : @growmentum

Made in the USA
Las Vegas, NV
07 July 2024